"*Surrender*—not a word we usua don't want to relinquish control. Kristen gives a realistic view of the challenges and joys of surrendering your life to Christ, what it means to let Him have control. She is honest about her journey, the times she did let Him have control as well as the times she walked her own path and the consequences of those decisions. We see not only the good but also the scars. Though it seems simple—just surrender— we are given a glimpse of how difficult that is because of our fallen nature and how the enemy wants to derail us. If you want to see the practical side of surrender and the reasons it brings life, this is a must read."

—Susie Edworthy,
International Mission Board emeritus missionary,
wife, mother, and grandmother

"Eating breakfast alone in a hotel restaurant in Amsterdam, a young man—a teenager—approached me and asked if he could sit at my table. He shared about his life living overseas. I remember thinking his mom should write a book about raising children. Just minutes ago, I finished her book. It's not a book about raising children. It's a book about a much more difficult topic: surrender. Kristen Hepner's voice shines through in her memoir. I felt like I was reading a personal letter from one of my best friends. Her book encouraged and comforted me as I was reminded that living a full life means surrendering every aspect of life to God. Reading this book will help you look at your life and see that living a life surrendered to the will of God really is the best life."

—Michelle Chitwood,
professional educator and mom, wife to Dr. Paul Chitwood,
president of the International Mission Board

"*Surrendering: My Story of Embracing the Will of God* is a beautiful testimony to the life of its author. Kristen Hepner has managed to share deeply and honestly, with humor and passion, her journey of living a life of surrender to a good God who is trustworthy. Her insights into God's Word, His character, and His love for His children are refreshing and challenging. I highly recommend this book for anyone who desires to grow spiritually and truly abide in Christ.

—Karen Pearce,
International Mission Board missionary,
disciple, wife, and mother

"Reading *Surrendering* is like having an honest conversation with a dear friend about what truly matters in life. Kristen Hepner shares candidly how the Lord has lovingly shaped and formed her along an incredible journey of life experiences. She shares biblical truth for every season of the heart and invites readers to take a deep look within at the state of their own souls. Through it all, Kristen maintains her declaration that God is worthy and that He is the One who is calling each one of us to live a life surrendered to Him."

—Elisabeth Boss,
affinity leader for European peoples at
International Mission Board, disciple, wife, and mom

"To know Kristen Hepner is to love her. Reading her book feels just like sitting down with her for a cup of coffee. I am impressed and humbled by her transparency and yet challenged and encouraged by her journey. Do not miss this opportunity to see what God can do with a life surrendered."

—Angela Carter,
minster of education and women's ministry at
Brushy Creek Baptist Church, Taylors, South Carolina

Surrendering

My Story of Embracing the Will of God

Kristen Hepner

LUCIDBOOKS

Surrendering
My Story of Embracing the Will of God

Copyright © 2020 by Kristen Hepner

Published by Lucid Books in Houston, TX
www.LucidBooksPublishing.com

All rights reserved. No part of this publication may be reproduced, stored in a retrieval system, or transmitted in any form by any means, electronic, mechanical, photocopy, recording, or otherwise, without the prior permission of the publisher, except as provided for by USA copyright law.

Unless otherwise indicated, all Scripture quotations are taken from the Holy Bible, New International Version®, NIV®. Copyright © 1973, 1978, 1984, 2011 by Biblica, Inc.™ Used by permission of Zondervan. All rights reserved worldwide. www.zondervan.com The "NIV" and "New International Version" are trademarks registered in the United States Patent and Trademark Office by Biblica, Inc.™

Scripture quotations marked (ESV) are taken from the ESV® Bible (The Holy Bible, English Standard Version®), copyright © 2001 by Crossway, a publishing ministry of Good News Publishers. Used by permission. All rights reserved.

Scripture quotations marked (ISV) are taken from the Holy Bible: International Standard Version®. Copyright © 1996-forever by The ISV Foundation. ALL RIGHTS RESERVED INTERNATIONALLY. Used by permission.

Scripture quotations marked (NASB) are taken from the New American Standard Bible® (NASB), Copyright © 1960, 1962, 1963, 1968, 1971, 1972, 1973, 1975, 1977, 1995 by The Lockman Foundation. Used by permission. www.lockman.org.

ISBN: 978-1-63296-417-5
eISBN: 978-1-63296-884-5

Special Sales: Most Lucid Books titles are available in special quantity discounts. Custom imprinting or excerpting can also be done to fit special needs. Contact Lucid Books at Info@LucidBooksPublishing.com.

This book is dedicated to my best friend, life partner, children's daddy, and adoring husband, Josh Hepner. Without you, I would have never found the confidence to put these stories on paper. I am so thankful that the Lord allowed me to be your favorite.

Table of Contents

Introduction

*The Lord G**OD** has given me the tongue of those who are taught, that I may know how to sustain with a word him who is weary. Morning by morning he awakens; he awakens my ear to hear as those who are taught.*

—Isa. 50:4 ESV

For years, it has been a dream of mine to write a book. But there was not a point in time when the thought came to me that it might be a good idea. I just knew that one day writing would be part of my world. I have never been trained as a writer, but the joy of being able to bless someone with my words is something I felt compelled to pursue. My prayer is that through my writing, I will point you to the feet of Jesus. My prayer is that my words will explain His goodness and faithfulness in such a way that you will be encouraged. My prayer is that this book will help you understand the joys of *surrendering* your entire life to Jesus Christ. He is worthy, faithful, and good.

My purpose for writing this book is to share with you the ins and outs of a life that has been surrendered to Christ. My hope is to tell you the story of a broken woman who found the most precious treasure known to humanity, who came to the place where she knew she could no longer live on her own strength and for her own purposes but was called to something better, something greater. It is the story of a woman who came to realize the difference between having a Savior and having a Lord who was greater than herself.

My story is one of real-life struggle. This life I live is blessed, yet I can become blinded by selfish longings, shattered earthly dreams, and pity pursuits that all leave me longing. Writing this book and telling my story is an attempt to relate to others and affirm that while life is hard and the struggle is real, we serve a God who is more than a conqueror. May He reign today, tomorrow, and forever in our present. May we learn to see Him in the ordinary, everyday things.

Often, I feel the need to sing an old hymn:

> Turn your eyes upon Jesus,
> Look full in His wonderful face,
> And the things of earth will grow strangely dim,
> In the light of His glory and grace.[1]

It helps me recenter and refocus on the only One who is worthy. I pray for myself and for you that surrendering to God will come more and more easily and naturally with each passing day.

Recently, I listened to Billy Graham's funeral. Wow! What a man of God who was chosen by God and undeniably used by Him all over the world. One pastor who spoke talked about the man

---

1. Helen Howarth Lemmel, "Turn Your Eyes upon Jesus," Hymnal.net, https://www.hymnal.net/en/hymn/h/645.

Graham was and the life he lived. He recalled a conversation when Graham asked him if he wanted a successful ministry. "Of course," the pastor answered, to which Graham responded, "Don't talk about yourself. Talk about Jesus."[2] What a knife through the heart. While I feel like writing this book was done out of obedience to the Lord, it feels as if it has certainly turned into a lot of stories about me. Hear my heart in this, though. I am nothing without Jesus. My heart in writing this book is to point people to the cross and to Jesus, who is the giver of life.

Many of us today go through life searching for purpose, yearning to be important even in one person's life. That is a God-given desire. He has written it into the DNA of each person throughout history, all with the end goal of making His name known. Choosing Him and surrendering your life to His will is the first step in finding your true purpose. Telling my story is my attempt to sing God's praises. Without Him, I would be nothing. With Him, I live an incredible life full of purpose and passion.

To live a life of surrendering is the greatest adventure anyone could ever experience. Many people believe that following Christ is a boring, mundane life filled with rules. I want to be the first to counter that lie. Living for Christ fills your life with adventure—heart-pounding adventures and rip-your-heart-out sorrows. Following the Lord will take you from the highest highs to the lowest lows and back again. The beautiful part of it all is allowing Jesus to seep into the marrow of each of those experiences.

I have found that the greatest challenge to overcome is myself. I am such a creature of habit and comfort, longing for what's easy. God has such wonderful works out there waiting for me, but I constantly stand in His way. It is so obvious to see the words written in Romans all over my life.

---

2. "Billy Graham 1918–2018 Funeral Service Transcript, BillyGraham.org, https://memorial.billygraham.org/funeral-service-transcript/.

I do not understand what I do. For what I want to do I do not do, but what I hate I do. And if I do what I do not want to do, I agree that the law is good. As it is, it is no longer I myself who do it, but it is sin living in me. For I know that good itself does not dwell in me, that is, in my sinful nature. For I have the desire to do what is good, but I cannot carry it out. For I do not do the good I want to do, but the evil I do not want to do—this I keep on doing. Now if I do what I do not want to do, it is no longer I who do it, but it is sin living in me that does it.

—Rom. 7:15–20

My point is that I surrendered enough of myself and the sin I hate to allow the Spirit to live in me and complete this manuscript.

As you read these stories, I pray that you see Jesus using a broken, common woman for the purpose of being a light in this dark world, a beacon to the lost. Trust me, He wants to use you, too. The choice is all yours—to live your life for yourself or to live a life *surrendering*.

CHAPTER 1

My Story: Unaware of Surrender

He who has found his life will lose it, and he who has lost
his life for My sake will find it.
—Matt. 10:39 NASB

Everyone has a story to tell. Hearing those stories is one of my favorite parts of getting to know new people. Some people like to be mysterious, which makes learning their story even more fun and challenging. Others are open books, and with a few good questions, they begin to divulge the depths of their hearts. Our stories shape who we are. They explain our worldview, beliefs, and morals; they also shape our perceptions of the day-to-day lives we live. Our life experiences, the culture that surrounds us, and even the time in history when we live all make up who we are and make our stories unique. No two are alike, which is one reason I love to hear other people's stories. What I especially love is the way God writes our stories. He is the best storyteller, and His way of writing peripeteia into our lives is mind-blowing.

Recently, I was introduced to the word *peripeteia*, and boy, do I love that word. It is defined as "a sudden or unexpected reversal of circumstances or situation especially in a literary work."[1] Our life is a story. Your story and mine were written by the God who created the oceans and the skies, the sunsets and the storms. Whether you realize it or not, you were created to live a life that brings glory to this amazing God. It is with our stories that we become lights on a hill and salt to the lost. It is with our stories that God is writing history and building His Kingdom. So remember what He has done, and tell your story.

It's difficult to know where to begin to tell the story of this Georgia girl who wound up in a small town in eastern Europe. The road has been long and sometimes bumpy, but Jesus—the foundation upon whom I have learned to build my life—has held firm in both doubt and storms.

Though my childhood wasn't perfect, I never doubted that I was loved—a blessing that I have undoubtedly taken for granted at times. It all started in a small, middle of Georgia town where my mom ended up after her father was stationed there with the special services department of the military. After living in a number of places, including Bermuda, my grandmother, better known to me as Mema, decided the family had done enough moving around and they would stay put. Mom was a teenager by then, and one day in high school, she met a boy named Jimmy who later became my daddy. He was said to be a kindhearted, life-of-the-party kind of guy and quite the ladies' man. Mom was smitten. Daddy was drafted, ordered to go to Germany, and went unwillingly. They later married when he was on leave in the United States and then both quickly boarded a plane to Germany. I think those months were sweet for both of them. Though

---

1. "peripeteia," *Merriam-Webster*, https://www.merriam-webster.com/dictionary/peripeteia.

I like the thought of getting married and being whisked off to a foreign land to learn how to live together, I also know it was difficult, for I have done it.

It's fun for me to try to piece together the stories and imagine what life was like for these two people who made me. It's fun to look through old pictures and imagine what the room felt like when someone took each one. I imagine dates and romantic evenings, lots of laughter, and silly moments in life. However, I have lived long enough to know that there were hard times, too. I have no doubt they experienced incredible highs and lows, as well as sweet times of sacrifice and hard times of selfishness. That's marriage.

By the time I came along, life was pretty settled for my parents. They were back in the States, Mom working as a secretary and Dad holding a steady job on the air force base in town. Life was good, and they enjoyed welcoming a baby girl into the family. Mom had suffered a miscarriage a few years before I was born, so I'm sure the heartbreak of that loss only increased the joy of my arrival. Late in November on Thanksgiving Day, Dad called Mema to tell her that Mom was in labor, although she thought he was kidding at first because he was known for always being the joker. Papa, my grandfather, was in a deer stand when something told him, "Laurie is going to have that baby today." It also happened to be his birthday. I was blessed to share my first 20 birthdays with my Papa, who always endearingly called me his little turkey.

Some of my favorite childhood memories are of a backyard, above-ground swimming pool, family dinners at Mema's house, Halloween with friends, helping Dad in his woodworking shop, and front porch swinging and singing at Mema's. It's funny how each of those descriptions takes me back to a time and feeling, a sweet memory of life as a child. I know that the mind has a way of holding on to the bad and more stressful times, but there were so many more good times. I often wonder what my children will remember. Will it be the wonderful times of laughter or the times I lost my temper and yelled? Will they remember the nights I came into their rooms to pray over them or the times I was too busy to tuck them in? I pray that, if nothing else, they know how very much I love them. My family did that for me.

Obviously, my story doesn't begin at the age of eight, but I usually seem to start there when sharing with others. It was then that a label was put on my life that I am still trying to shrug off—the label of "innocent victim." I became the innocent victim of a crime that crushed dreams, took a life, and changed the future for so many people I love. My father was murdered in a horrible crime when I was eight years old. My innocence was shattered. The reality of sin became personal; loss and confusion ensued.

I have relived that story many times from many different perspectives. I think of the unfairness of a life taken too early; Dad had so much more that he wanted to do. I contemplate the heart of my mama, who ached and grieved and had to learn to live without her husband. The older I get, the more I understand the pain she lived through. I think of my aunts who had to say goodbye to a brother they loved and needed. I mourn for my grandmother who had to bury her son; she was a woman left with only memories that would haunt her until the day she went to heaven. We were a family torn apart way before its time. I think of all Daddy's friends who experienced up close how short life can be. Many were left with the regret of not having just one more chance to speak with Dad before he died. "The heart knows its own bitterness, and no stranger shares its joy" (Prov. 14:10 ESV). Each one who is touched by such a loss has a personal story through the complicated world of grief.

Then there's me. I was Daddy's only child. It's surprising that my first thoughts go to how his death affected others. But when I ponder how it affected me, I think that is when I developed a need to please others and make them happy. I remember being confused and afraid and wondering how this could have happened. Afraid that I might die, too, and concerned about how my loved ones would get through Daddy's passing were strong emotions. I think the grieving process for a child manifests itself in many ways, and the weight of the loss is somehow minimized because children cannot fully understand the immensity of the tragedy. Perhaps the Lord simply guards and protects His little ones and truly does pull us into the shadow of His wings.

Dad's death was a loss that defined me—in the way of a title more than something like losing a limb. The title came from family, from school, even from counseling. I had a reason to be sad, mad, frustrated, or out of control. I wasn't any of those. In fact, most of the time, I was sweet, nice, kind, and even-tempered, but I do remember sometimes hitting emotional walls throughout my childhood. Everyone always pointed back to the loss of my father and gave that as the reason, my excuse to get out of line and display bad behavior. My father was murdered, for heaven's sake. I was a victim. What I really needed was to be filled with the love, grace, and purpose of my heavenly Father. I would not meet Him for quite a few years yet, but nevertheless, I was His chosen one, and He was, indeed, with me.

Years later, I came to realize that the title I assumed—victim—was going to be a lifelong struggle, a battle to not live my life as someone out of control. It's taken me years and the help of a counselor to put my finger on that. It began as a truth; I was truly a victim to a horrible crime, but over the years that truth manifested itself into a manipulative and yucky excuse. Rather than just being an identity, role, or title I could wear, receive pity for, and then take off, it became almost a need, an expectation of what I needed from others that always left me feeling shamed and empty. It affected the simplest and most complicated of my relationships. It affected my thoughts and feelings about the world, myself, and others. It became a habitual coping mechanism I would use to feel sorry for myself and give myself excuses for acting or behaving in a very ungodly way.

It's so sad how just plain evil the devil is. He takes pains and wounds from a place of pure innocence and uses them in our hearts and minds if we allow him to do so. The unfortunate thing is that most of us don't realize the ammunition he has collected over the years. But he knows. He knows exactly what situations can be turned into the fiery dart needed to turn us into bitter, selfish people, to be blind in our own minds to the pain we may be causing others. The master of deceit and the father of lies is the one who makes us hypocrites—well-meaning yet blinded hypocrites. You know you are blind to it all when you read Matthew's words: "You hypocrite, first take the plank out of your own eye, and then you will see clearly to remove the speck from your brother's eye" (Matt. 7:5). The first thought you have is "Yeah! Take that, you judgmental person!" However, you neglect to see yourself in there. I say that because I know. I was there. I often joke with one of my best friends about how easy it is to become prideful in your self-*less*-ness. Hypocritical? Maybe just a little.

Mom and I moved around trying to find our place in the world after Dad's death. It was a difficult time for Mom, but she did a great job making me feel like a normal kid. When I was 10, she went to work as a secretary for a man who later became my stepfather. I wasn't sure about Bob from the beginning. Mom and I were so close, and it felt scary to let someone else into that circle. Bob did a good job of easing into our lives because I don't remember being resentful or disliking him. He didn't try to take the place of my father. He loved my mother and was there. Our relationship has always been civil but not deep. I don't know why that is, maybe because of the man he is—quiet, reserved, tranquil. Or perhaps it was because of the wild spirit I was that he didn't know what to do with me. Don't hear me saying that we had a bad relationship because that wasn't the case; we just didn't have a close one until much later in life.

When I was 12, Bob got a job in Athens, Georgia, and my mother and I moved there with him. The move took me away from not only everything familiar in my world but also Mema and Papa. I was devastated. Home to me was always where Mema and Papa lived, in a little trailer that had been turned into a house. They were safe and secure and always there. It was a move that was hard on my entire family.

They say there is a silver lining to every cloud, and this move had one for me. Moving to Athens and beginning school in Oconee County caused my life's destiny to collide with the man who would become my life partner. I met Josh, my unknown-to-me-at-the-time Prince Charming on the day I started seventh grade.

Middle school and high school were some of the darkest days of my life. I was lost from the Lord and had no clue what my identity was outside of being pretty. I wanted to feel loved, accepted, and popular. Unfortunately, I chose every avenue to achieve all those titles. Boys, alcohol, drugs, partying—been there, done that. I was lost and confused and a complete mess.

When I was 16, problems began at home. In my mind, life was all about having fun, numbing the hard situations, and making it to the next party. This particular time was neither fun nor pretty. By the age of 17, halfway through my senior year of high school, I found myself living on my own. My apartment became a party place, and my life felt hopeless and lonely. It was a deeply painful time. It is hard for me to think about those months with much fondness, but somehow I made it through with relatively few scars. I think one of the reasons was because I did have a great group of friends, mostly boys, who loved me deeply. I think they saw the sweet spirit and heart I had buried inside and felt sorry for the girl I was fumbling through life trying to be. One of those friends was Josh Hepner—I called him Buddy.

I am smiling like a teenage girl as I write this—well, maybe I have more of a smirk on my face. Buddy was this huge guy on the football team who gave the best hugs in the world. He loved me dearly, but not in the way the other boys did. He saw my heart and, in typical Josh style, just wanted to help by telling me what an idiot I was. He was convinced that I could do much better and needed to make some changes. It took me many years to realize how much

I loved him. It would take me even longer to realize how much my heavenly Father loved me, but the story isn't over yet. God had a plan, and I would one day choose to surrender.

The beginning of my story is not the beginning I would have chosen. However, the older I get, the more I realize that we don't get to choose the peripeteia of our stories. What we can choose is how we react to the parts of our story that are not picture-pretty. In Genesis is this promise: "As for you, you meant evil against me, but God meant it for good" (Gen. 50:20 ESV). Does that mean God could bring good out of the murder of my father? Yes, it does. I may not understand that good this side of heaven, but I trust in the One who writes my story.

As you think about the beginning of your own story, what emotions come to the surface? Are they happy emotions of blissful, carefree moments? If so, thank God for His protection over your life. Maybe the emotions you feel are sad or bitter. If this is the case, surrender those hurts to Jesus. His burden is light (Matt. 11:29). Walking around wearing a face that screams, "Life is hard, and I am a victim," makes people want to run in the other direction. Healing can be had from even the deepest wounds. Allow the Lord to heal you. It is refreshment to your body and nourishment to your bones (Prov. 3:8).

I was unaware of the need to surrender my life to Jesus. Are you aware of the importance of making a decision to trust and follow Jesus? Do you know that you were created for a purpose and God has a great plan for your life? God loved you so much that He sent His Son, Jesus, to this earth to live a perfect life and then die as a sacrifice for us all. Freedom is waiting for you—freedom from sin and shame, freedom from death, and the promise of eternal life. "He who has found his life will lose it, and he who has lost his life for My sake will find it" (Matt. 10:39 NASB).

CHAPTER 2

Our Love Story; Cords of Surrender

*"For I know the plans I have for you," declares the L*ORD*,
"plans to prosper you and not to harm you, plans to give
you hope and a future."*
—Jer. 29:11

This is one of my favorite stories to tell. I am such a romantic at heart. And boy, do I have an amazing love story. It's one that could have been written only by the One who is love Himself. God chose two very broken and unlikely candidates to write a love story that would continue to be awe-inspiring to anyone who hears it. I know that sounds dramatic, but it kind of is, or maybe I am just the dramatic one.

From the time Josh and I met in Mrs. Karakoff's seventh-grade homeroom, we have had a bond. Thankfully, it has always been true kindness and genuine love that knitted our hearts together. We were able to build a friendship on top of pure and innocent intentions. From day one, that is what we did—build a strong friendship.

Every now and then we find a note one of us wrote to the other in our terrible middle school handwriting and folded in that special way that the paper creates an envelope and tucks into itself all nice and tidy. We wrote about nothing, telling the other one to "call me" or "wait on me in the bus line." We asked questions that demanded a check in a yes or no box. We sat together at lunch and lined up together on the way to art class. There was even a season when I picked him up on the way to the church we attended, just to hang out. At a very early age, I knew his family, and he knew mine.

Around the age of 16, I was close enough to his family to start going on family vacations with them. We went to places like Myrtle Beach, South Carolina, and Panama City, Florida, for a week over the summer. I have wonderful memories of lying out in the sun on the beach with Josh's mother and going out to dinner with his dad. Josh and I have memories of haunted houses, race cars, and putt-putt golf that we enjoyed together just as friends. I see those years as God's blessing to us. When the time came for us to take another direction in our relationship, we had already built a solid friendship. I am very close to 40 years old now, and I still consider him my best friend, and he considers me his biggest cheerleader. What a gift from God—a gift that was given before we ever knew who God was.

God gives good gifts, and His plans prevail over anything we could plan for ourselves. He chose Josh and me before time ever began, and He had our story, as well as your story, written well before we ever knew it. That is what is so exciting about looking back and even looking forward. "Teach me Your way, O Lord, that I may walk in your truth; unite my heart to fear your name" (Ps. 86:11 ESV).

High school quickly came and went. We had both dated around but always considered stepping out of the friend zone to the off-limits area in our relationship. I remember one time when we were riding down the road in his white Ford Bronco (he still misses that thing), going nowhere, like usual, I had the thought, *I should kiss him.* Hear me out. That would be like saying you wanted to kiss your very best friend. It was an odd thought. To this day, because I shared that tidbit of information with him, he says it was me who initiated that first kiss.

Senior prom came and went. We both had other dates. I remember feeling a little bitter that he wouldn't take me, but he had a girlfriend at the time, so it was only fair that he took her. I went with a friend, and we had a great time. Soon after was graduation. Josh had planned for months to go out west with a couple of his buddies. They were mad when he skipped out on them and instead went with me and a huge group of fellow graduates to Cancun, Mexico, for a few days to kick off our last summer together. Remember, we did not know the Lord at the time.

It was there on an elevator at a resort hotel in Mexico that the stars aligned, and we crossed the friends-only zone. We kissed. I say that he kissed me, and he says that I kissed him. Maybe it was just the Tequila talking, but either way, we passed the point of no return, far away from the friend zone.

Our original plan was to keep that week in Cancun just that—in Cancun. That lasted all of four hours. From the beginning, it felt right, and we fell deeply in love that summer. Those few months together could be a blockbuster movie because they were magical. We spent every minute that we could together. Many of our friends were mad at us for crossing the line and becoming more than just friends. We didn't care; we were together, and nothing else mattered.

At that time, we had both already made decisions about which colleges we were going to attend in the fall, so we squeezed everything we could out of that one summer and made the most of it. I don't think we were apart for more than a few hours at a time. The memories we made during those months still bring a smile to my face several decades later.

The time came for us to pack up and head off to college. It was heart-wrenching, but we promised each other that somehow, some way, we were going to make it work. And we did.

That first year was a doozy for me, especially in the fall during football season. I traveled from southern Georgia to South Carolina and beyond to watch my man play football. Some weekends, I traveled eight hours one way just to watch him play on Saturday, spend Saturday night and Sunday morning with him, and then drive back in time to get some decent sleep on Sunday night. I still remember those goodbyes. They were painful. Any of you who have experienced a long-distance relationship have been there. God protected us, even though we did not honor Him at the time. He kept us safe both from others and from ourselves. We remained faithful to each other, and for that, I am forever grateful.

We spent the next summer living together in Athens, Georgia, and the following fall, I transferred to a college that was located as far north as possible yet still in Georgia so I could keep my state-funded scholarship. Again, we struggled with the long-distance thing, but we made it work. We were committed, but just when we thought it might be too hard, the hand of God intervened. On February 7, 2001, I found out I was pregnant.

Looking back, the pregnancy is what held us together during those months. We were not living within God's great plan of saving ourselves for marriage, nor were we committed to serving the Lord with our lives. Quite the opposite was true. We were living our lives fully for ourselves. The Bible tells us that it is the Lord who opens and closes the womb. While we were the ones who were acting outside of His will, He is the one who allowed us to conceive. Who knows the paths we would have taken without Dayne entering our lives. I believe God intervened in our unsurrendered lives to ultimately bring us to Himself. That's food for thought.

I'll never forget the feeling of frantically taking that first pregnancy test, the second, and then the third and the fourth; of driving to the health department just to make sure and crying hysterically as the nurse told me that everything was going to be okay but feeling that *nothing* was. I remember calling my mom—just to hear her voice—and without saying a word, I heard her ask me, "Honey, are you pregnant?"

Josh. What would I tell him? He was a star football player. He had his entire future at his fingertips. Would he even want this baby? It was such a hard time. I told him on the phone. I was a mess. The conversation wasn't the most romantic, so I will skip those details. Let's just say we were both shocked—and terrified.

Again, looking back with the Holy Spirit now living inside me, I can see God's hand on us. We live in a time when abortion is said to be a quick fix for a little "accident" like pregnancy. The pain and scars of abortion that plague our nation may be very personal to you, and if they are, I want you to believe that there is forgiveness and healing in Jesus. I believe that God protected us from walking that road, and we will forever be thankful that the thought of abortion never crossed our minds. That, my friends, is the Lord. I can give glory to no other. Just the thought of not having my son here today is enough to stop me in my tracks.

We both finished up that spring semester of our sophomore year before moving in together that summer. We lived in Athens with Josh's mom. It was a tough time. I was mad that I was pregnant and couldn't go on with the partying lifestyle we enjoyed, and Josh was trying to live it up and get it all out before the baby came. It wasn't a great time in the life of us, but we made it.

Josh proposed that summer. It was a perfect summer day on the river. We had been playing in the water all day and ended up sitting on some old train trestles positioned over the river. I remember how nervous he was; he was visibly shaking. I don't think I have ever seen him so nervous since that moment. It was perfect. I said yes, of course, but wanted to wait until after the baby was born to actually get married. I think I wanted to wait because I didn't want to be pregnant at my wedding. I know. It's a lame excuse, but it is the truth.

Finally, the day came for us to welcome our son. He was the most beautiful little thing either one of us had ever seen. We were smitten. Josh's best friend, an aspiring songwriter, came to visit and shared a song with us that he had written for our son, Dayne. The chorus contained this phrase: "Our miracle in disguise, our favorite mistake." The entire song was spot on, exactly how we felt. The most wonderful thing was that God was never surprised for one minute. Dayne's days were written in time at the beginning of creation. God had a perfect and beautiful plan for him. I am honored that I got to be there at the first purpose of that sweet baby boy's life, to wake up his mom and dad from their life of stupidity.

After Dayne was born, Josh had an experience in the nursery late one night that changed his life forever. We were both high after a night of partying when Josh walked into Dayne's room to check on him. To this day when he tells this story, he gets chill bumps up and down his arms. He had an encounter with the Lord that night. He says that as he looked at his newborn son, he heard the Lord speak to him as clear as day. "Josh, what are you doing?" He knew what he needed to do. He understood at that moment that it was time for him to put his childish ways behind him and be the man God was calling him to be. From that moment, Josh allowed God to be Lord of his life.

We were married in June 2002 at a small chapel in Gatlinburg, Tennessee, surrounded by 50 of our closest family members and friends. The entire event cost us $1,000. On the home front, we were struggling—both of us trying to finish college, raise a baby, work a few jobs, and make this new marriage work. Honestly, we were in a rough place, but praise Jesus, we made it.

A few more months would pass before I surrendered my life to the Lord.

Looking back at this story is bittersweet. It is bitter because we lived in sin. And as much as we love Jesus now and live our lives for

Him, sin leaves a sting. Hear that. I would love for young people to learn from mistakes we made. One of my fears has always been that people would look at our lives and say, "Look, they had their fun and turned out okay." Yes, by the grace of God, we did turn out okay; but the sin we lived through left its scars. Scars run deep and are always there to remind us. Jesus's blood is sufficient to cover us and wipe those sins away as far as the east is from the west (Ps. 103:12). He is enough. All the time. However, sin has consequences. Always.

Think about Moses in the Bible. He was a stud. He went before the Egyptian Pharaoh numerous times, walked through the 10 plagues as God's chosen leader, led the Israelites out of bondage, and parted the Red Sea. He went on to record God's Levitical law and the Ten Commandments, build the tabernacle, and beg God for mercy time and again for those silly, complaining Israelites. We talk about the patience of Job, but I would suggest we should have the patience of Moses. The dude put up with a lot. Then one day, when those people were complaining again that they were going to die of thirst, Moses went before the Lord and asked for provisions for God's people. God told him to *speak* to the rock and tell it to bring forth water. Moses did what God said, sort of. Instead of *speaking* to the rock, he *struck* it—and did not give credit to the Lord for providing the water. His punishment? God prohibited him from entering the Promised Land, something Moses had been looking forward to his whole life. Sin has consequences. Never choose it.

As I write these words, we are more than 17 years into our marriage. I love who God has made my husband into even more than I loved the boy who stole my heart. I recently had the opportunity to minister to a young, new mother who is going through a very difficult time in her marriage. She doesn't know the Lord yet. I am praying hard for her. Going into the meeting, I prayed fervently. I wanted to be sure I made the point of God's influence in our marriage. In all honesty, Josh and I would not be together today without the power of Jesus in our lives. I wanted her to know that. She and her husband have commented many times over the past few years how much they love us, respect our marriage, and appreciate the way we raise our kids. We have told them time and again that we have simply followed God's plan in all those things. What a beautiful testimony that He uses us and our marriage as a beacon in a lost world.

As we talked, I did my best to point her to the only worthy solution—Jesus. I also felt led to leave her with these three thoughts, or pieces of advice, that I have learned over the years. I told her to pray for her man. When all else fails, I pray for Josh. When I try to focus on changing him or fixing him, I take my eyes off the only One who is capable of changing a person. We have to pray for our spouses. Next, I encouraged her to forgive him. Forgive him for mean words, unmet expectations, and everything in between. Holding a grudge or making a list of wrongs is detrimental to a marriage. Forgive your spouse. Finally, I told her to remember—remember what it was like when they first came together. Remember the feelings and emotions, the sweet words and gestures. Listen to music to help you remember; look at pictures to help you remember. Memories are a beautiful blessing from the Lord.

As I sit here and remember the beginnings of us, I smile. We are so very blessed to have been chosen by the Savior of the world to live a life of Kingdom purpose. I thank the Lord every day for the man He created for me. I am thankful that Josh lives a life surrendered to the Lord, and we daily continue to surrender our lives and marriage to the lordship of Jesus. After all, Ecclesiastes 4:12 tells us, "Though one may be overpowered, two can defend themselves. A cord of three strands is not quickly broken."

CHAPTER 3

My Call: Surrendering to Obedience

Then I heard the voice of the Lord saying,
"Whom shall I send? And who will go for us?" And I said,
"Here am I. Send me!"

—Isa. 6:8

We had no clue. We had no clue what it meant to walk with Jesus or to look like Him. We were such babies, both in years and maturity. Sure, we had tasted what the world had to offer, had a child, thought we were grown up, but we were so clueless. The beautiful thing about this is that we also had no idea how to play the part in the Christian dance. In other words, from day one, we were teachable and transparent. We had no idea that many in the church wore masks most days. I realize that statement might at first seem to be a cynical spirit, but I want to be real.

We laugh about it now, how gullible we were. The Holy Spirit had so much work to do in us, and He wasted no time. Shortly after praying to receive Christ, I locked eyes with a young woman at college chapel one day. In that moment, I saw a woman strong in the Lord; she was everything I wanted to become. She heard the Holy Spirit whisper to her heart, "Teach her." We simply smiled at each other, knowing that the Lord had plans for both of us. She was so strong in the Lord and had been for as long as she could remember. The previous two years of history in her life versus mine were the farthest apart on the spectrum that two lives could be. Mine was pursuing worldly passions and desires, longing for love and finding it in all the wrong places. Hers was knowing who she was in Christ, feeling fully loved and alive and striving to be more like Him every day. Taking me on as a disciple was such a risk for her. I was a wayward soul who had walked many miles in a life ridden with sin. Yet she discipled me with such love and grace and strength. I remember so clearly asking her many questions during those first few weeks and months. Is drinking coffee a sin? What does it mean to dress modestly? What does it look like to walk with Jesus?

She was precious and gentle in her answers. I have no doubt she saw a teachable spirit and a life truly and completely surrendered. It reminds me of the bean my daughter just planted. She actually soaked it in blue food coloring first, and the bean turned from white to blue. It was for some type of science experiment that I won't even pretend I remember. She then planted the bean just to see what would happen, and lo and behold, a plant popped up, and yes, it produced a small plant that had blue parts. The small plant was fragile and had been stained by all that it sat in. It reminded me of myself. I was small, fragile, and a little bit stained, but because I had finally been planted, God was changing me into something He could use.

By that time, Josh had also surrendered his life to the lordship of Jesus. While we were both trying to figure out what that meant, we were finally on the same page. We had a baby, we were working as many jobs as we could, and we were trying our best to finish college. Josh played football throughout high school and college, and the Lord would go on to use his love and talent for the game in our lives in the future, but more about that later.

Again, we didn't know much, but what we did know was that we should go to church. We were hippies, so we put on our best Birkenstocks and hemp necklaces and went to church. The church we originally drove to had a full parking lot. When we read on the sign that it had already started, we drove down the road a short distance to what is now our home church. I know what you are thinking— oh good, they found a church. However, let me clarify. We found a family. We had no idea what it meant to be loved and supported by the body of Christ like our church family loved and supported us. The love we have for our church family is *big*. They have been with us from day one of our walk with the Lord.

On that first Sunday morning, we walked up to this soon-to-be-family place and were greeted by a man who would become our so-called spiritual father. He was a very conservative man with a genuine smile. He seemed to look past our rugged appearance to see two people who were hungry for Jesus. He asked us what our story was, so for the first time, we told him how we were living a life of pleasure for ourselves and how we were now dedicating our lives to live for God. We had *no* idea of the implications of that statement, but we saw it was important, as this man we had just met began to cry.

Fast-forward a few months, and we were all in, reading the Word on our own, attending church several times a week, being trained in how to share our faith, and signing up for mission trips. On a personal level, it was a hard time for some of our friends and family. We were so different, and everyone around us saw it. To them we must have seemed like judgmental snobs, but in reality, we had tasted the Lord and seen that He was good. We were done with our old way of life.

We laugh now at how naive we were. We were like children, completely teachable. If the preacher or a trusted teacher would have said, "Jump," we would have asked how high. When the preacher said to give sacrificially to missions, guess what we did? We gave. When we were challenged to go on at least one mission trip per year, we packed our bags. And that is how it all started—being obedient to very godly counsel for which we are still grateful today. Men like Ralph Carter, Gary Wheeler, Brian Hartsell, and Phil Charping are just a few of the ones who helped open our eyes to the plan the Lord had for us.

One of the highlights of our year was going to New York City on a mission trip. The trip was a wonderful experience and is still being held today, led by an organization called Spread Truth Ministries. If you are interested in seeing how the Lord can radically open your eyes, check it out. The trip proved to be very fruitful for Josh and me. Collectively, our group would lead 30 to 40 people, sometimes more, to the Lord in one week. We were trained to use two approaches. One was setting up prayer stations. We went out in the mornings in groups of eight to 10 to strategic places around the city, carrying massive amounts of stuff with us. We had tables, Bibles, tracts, bright red banners that said Prayer Station, and matching red aprons that read Prayer Changes Things. We were sometimes in very busy subway hubs, while other times we were stationed in compact residential parts of the city. As people walked by, we asked them if we could pray with them. Sometimes they didn't even look our way, but other times, they accepted our offer.

In our training, we were told to say a brief prayer about whatever it was they needed prayer for. I prayed with people for things like the healing of a sick uncle, a daughter close to divorce, a sore toe, and financial struggles. You name it, and we would pray for God's hand to come into that situation. As soon as we said a brief prayer, we said, "Can I ask you a question?" Often, out of gratitude for the prayer, people almost automatically responded, "Sure."

At that point, using the Evangelism Explosion type of questioning in which we were trained, we began to share with them the best news in the world—that there is a God out there who loves them and has a plan for their lives, and that He gave His Son, Jesus, as a gift to the whole world. We explained that it wasn't enough to just know the present existed but that one had to truly receive that gift, to take that present off the shelf, open it, and receive the gift of eternal life by allowing Jesus to take their place and be the atonement for their sin. It was a beautiful week of watching many dead people come to life.

Have you taken a step of faith like that? Have you asked Jesus into your heart to be your Savior and Lord? You know that He died for you, too, because He loves you. If you have not surrendered your life to Christ, I would greatly encourage you to do so. He is the way, the truth, and the life (John 14:6), the only way to God. No amount of good deeds can earn your way to heaven. You can never be a good enough person. The Bible tells us in Matthew 5:48, "Be perfect, therefore, as your heavenly Father is perfect." I am sure that you have come to the point in your life that you understand that perfection is not achievable; I know I have. If you are still a skeptic of the Bible, read it. After all, it is the best seller of all time and has been around for a few years. It would be hard to consider yourself a cultured and knowledgeable person if you've never read the Bible. Give it a go. I dare ya!

Let's return to my time in New York City. During those days of my life, God gave me a heart to maintain contact with anyone I led to the Lord. I asked for their address (in those days, we still used snail mail), and I would write to them after returning home to South Carolina. I sent letters of encouragement, including scripture verses that meant something to me, and kept them updated with news from my family. It became part of my ministry to stay in contact with those new brothers and sisters. Sometimes they would write back, and the relationship would continue. Sometimes the Lord would use those letters for an even greater purpose.

One day in the fall of 2005, a few months after returning from a New York City trip, I received a phone call from someone named Betty, asking me how I knew her mother, Guadeloupe. Immediately, I was taken back to the streets of New York, standing there in my red apron praying with people, when an older Hispanic lady approached me.

"Hello. Is there anything I can pray about with you today?" I asked.

With eyes full of hope, she said, "Yes! I would like to pray to ask Jesus into my heart."

My heart skipped a few beats as I asked her what made her come to that decision. She explained to me that the day before she had stopped on this same street corner to have a man pray with her about a situation in her life, and he explained to her that Jesus had died for her sins. She went on to tell me that she had not slept at all that night, thinking about all the wonderful things he had explained to her, and she was so excited to come back today to pray and ask Jesus to come into her heart. Of course, we prayed, and with tears streaming down her face, Guadeloupe became a new woman.

Fast-forward several months to my phone call with her daughter, Betty. She was calling me because her mother had recently passed away after many years of battling AIDS. As Betty was cleaning out her mother's apartment, she found what she described as a very nice letter from a lady in South Carolina, and she wanted to know how I had met her mother. Now, let's just pause here for a minute. On a very human level, what do you say? I remember feeling overwhelmed and inadequate, silently praying in my heart that the Lord would give me the right words to say to this grieving daughter. In all honesty, I do not remember everything I said, but I do remember telling Betty how I had met her mother on the streets of New York City and shared the good news of Jesus Christ with her. I also had the privilege of encouraging her that even though her loss was great, she had the opportunity to see her mother again in heaven one day.

· I wish I could have recorded that phone call. I pray that I also shared with Betty the good news of Jesus. But I have no idea how the rest of the phone call went. My memories from that phone call are filled with awe, unworthiness, and even fear that I did not say the right things. However, regardless of how much I potentially messed it up for Betty, the Lord used that phone call to radically change me.

On a personal level, my life was complicated. My wonderful, amazing, godly, *adventurous* husband had recently gotten it into his head that God was calling our family to overseas missions. *What? Are you serious? That is just his adventurous spirit! It could not be of the Lord! Sell everything? Take my babies to Africa? No, thank you! I am just fine right here!* We had worked so hard to pull ourselves out of a life of sin, poverty, debt, and more. We had finally just arrived—new house, cars, babies, college graduates, careers. We were completely involved in the life of the church. We had all we needed, and it was a wonderful life. I was terrified. I was scared of Josh and his desire, and I was afraid of what the Lord was going to ask of me. I really hated the idea. Nothing about it appealed to me. Adventure? Who cares? New country? No, thank you. Following the Lord? Can't we do that from here?

It was a very stressful time. Josh learned to just be quiet and pray, but I knew he was always thinking about it. And so was I. The Lord was softly calling. It started off quietly but then got louder and louder. It got to the point that in every sermon I heard, God was calling us to missions (but the sermon had nothing to do with missions). Every song I listened to on the radio made my heart sing of the nations. My flesh cried—even screamed—no! But I was beginning to believe that Josh was right; the Lord was calling us.

The call from Betty about Guadelupe certainly pointed my heart back to God and His desire for our lives, but not quite enough, yet.

Usually, I am one who needs more confirmation than others. To this day, it's a running joke between Josh and me about how many times I lay out my fleece. Do you know that story? In the book of Judges, Gideon is seeking a confirmation from God.

> *Then Gideon said to God, "If you will save Israel by my hand, as you have said, behold, I am laying a fleece of wool on the threshing floor. If there is dew on the fleece alone, and it is dry on all the ground, then I shall know that you will save Israel by my hand, as you have said." And it was so. When he rose early next morning and squeezed the fleece, he wrung enough dew from the fleece to fill a bowl with water. Then Gideon said to God, "Let not your anger burn against me; let me speak just once more. Please let me test just once more with the fleece. Please let it be dry on the fleece only, and on all the ground let there be dew." And God did so that night; and it was dry on the fleece only, and on all the ground there was dew* (Judges 6:36–40 ESV).

So many things about this story bless my heart so much. I love how specific Gideon made his entreaties. He left no room for coincidence. I love how Gideon reminds God of what he has already heard Him speak, as if God needs reminding. I love how Gideon does this *twice* and how he uses the *same* situation with a little twist. Most of all, I love how God honors his requests and confirms what Gideon already knows.

However, a few things also bother me about this story. Where is Gideon's faith without seeing? Where is Gideon's confidence in himself? In God? How on earth did he have enough gumption to question the God of the universe?

Yeah, well, that is me. Sometimes I lack faith and just need to be sure. I often lack confidence in myself, and He so graciously reminds me of who I am. I need to lay it out a few times to be sure. Some, including my man, may call that a lack of faith. But you know what? God and I have this thing. I need more assurance, and by golly, He is faithful to give it to me. Most major life decisions that I know are from the Lord come in pairs (it's our thing) and I am so thankful He loves me enough to not give up on me.

Two weeks after my call from Betty, I received another phone call. This time, it was the daughter of a man named Jimmy. Again, I was taken back to Central Park several months earlier to a conversation I had with an older man on a park bench. He was such a nice-looking, smaller-framed man with white hair and the kindest eyes. I still remember him vividly to this day. He was just enjoying the day when this young, naive girl came his way. He really didn't want to talk but was too kind to refuse me. This time I was taking spiritual surveys, asking various questions to see where he stood in relation to God. He politely agreed to take the survey. As I sat beside him and learned that his name was Jimmy, I knew we had a connection. My daddy's name was Jimmy, and this man was close to the same age Daddy would have been had he still been alive. I know that Jimmy didn't pick his name, but I know that my heavenly Father allowed me to have a special moment with this man who shared a name with a man who meant so much to me. I love that God used a man named Jimmy to be my final fleece in a life-altering decision that was coming my way.

We talked about religion. We talked about the hypocrisy he had seen in the church his entire life. We talked about the differences between Catholics and Protestants. And we talked a lot about Jesus. In the end, Jimmy wanted Jesus. He did not want religion and hypocrisy. He did not want denomination and didn't want to be categorized. He did want the gift of salvation and eternal life that Jesus was offering him. He prayed and became a new man.

It was time for me to go, but it was so important for me to get his address so I could write to him. I could see the walls going up around his heart. He was *not* up for giving me his address. "You will take time out of your day to write me, and then I will feel obligated to write you back, and I just don't want that," he admitted.

I reassured him that he would never have to write me, that I would not expect even one letter.

By the time I received that phone call from his daughter six months later, I had five or six typed letters from his typewriter in my drawer. We became good friends. So when his daughter called me to tell me he had fallen down a flight of stairs, had a brain aneurysm, and died, my heart broke. She had been cleaning out her father's apartment and found many letters from a young woman in South Carolina. "How did you know my father?" Of course, I told her. I told her with a knot in my throat. I was devastated over her loss and over mine. I also knew that this was it; this was God's final call to me. It was time for me to give my life to telling people about Jesus. Enough making excuses; the call was crystal clear. I had to go, and I had to go now. People were dying. God had laid out my *two* fleeces. It was time for me to obey.

The very next Sunday, Josh and I went before our church congregation and dedicated our lives to full-time international missions. I couldn't see through all the tears that just wouldn't stop coming. I was in a full-on ugly cry. I knew it was totally of the Lord, but I was terrified of getting out of the boat like Jesus told Peter to do in Matthew 14. All I knew was that taking no action would have been sin for us.

Have you ever heard a bit of truth from someone that just stuck with you? I once heard the gospel being shared to a group of children by a lady who is like a mom to me. She is probably one of the best evangelists I've ever seen in action, especially when it comes to children. That day, I heard her explain sin to the kids. She said something like this: Sin is anything we do, say, or think that is contrary or against the will of God. Sin can also happen when you do *not* do something God has asked or commanded you to do.

There you have it—the sin of omission. How many times have I been guilty of that one? Too many to count. But there are some miraculous moments when I lay down my will for His and I get it right. This was one of those times. I knew without a shadow of a doubt that God was calling our family into full-time international missions. It had nothing to do with what I wanted in life. It was not on some bucket list of fantasies. It was not my people-pleasing self simply giving in to my husband's desires. It was a direct message for me and to me—to go.

God has a sense of humor. We found out that same Sunday night that we were going to have baby number three, Darcie Ann.

CHAPTER 4

The Land of Milk and Honey: Surrendering Dreams

*Trust in the LORD with all your heart and lean not on
your own understanding; in all your ways submit to him,
and he will make your paths straight.*

—Prov. 3:5–6

The day I prayed to receive Jesus as my Lord and Savior seems like yesterday in some ways. It began after dropping off our son Dayne at daycare. As full-time students at our college, we were required to attend chapel services twice per week. My husband had failed that requirement in his freshman year. On the drive to campus, I vividly remember a sense of anxious anticipation as I puffed on what would be my last cigarette. Somehow, something in me knew that my life was about to radically and completely change. I do not remember feeling afraid in any way, but I do remember sensing that something outside of myself— something bigger than me—was about to take place.

Memories flood my mind as I think about this destiny-altering day. Sitting in the chapel at North Greenville College, I sat in anticipation as I listened to a sermon. Josh was sitting beside me. I wish I could remember the preacher or the passage in the sermon, but I don't. The things I do remember are the wild beat of my heart and, as the altar call ensued, practically running to the front in an ugly cry (I have those a lot) knowing that the hole the preacher was talking about, the one that was Jesus's responsibility to fill, still existed in my heart. I needed it filled. A young woman, appropriately named Grace, stood waiting at the front of the chapel. That day she spoke profound truth to me and led me into the arms of Jesus. For years, I wanted to find her to tell her how much her words meant to me, how they have clung to me all these years. Finally, I reached out to her and was excited that she remembered me and that special moment.

I had dabbled in matters of faith before. You know what I mean. I had prayed the prayer of salvation every time I heard it, and I'd sung "Jesus Loves Me" in dark times when I was afraid. There was even a time in college when I thought about becoming a Buddhist as I naively learned about the Dalai Lama and the perusal of inner peace. In reality, I was lost, a lost soul in desperate need of a Savior.

That day in chapel with more than 1,000 students present, I knew for the first time what I needed to do. I needed to surrender my life to Jesus Christ. I needed to allow Him to take it all—my life, my plans, my dreams, my future, even my past, which included my sins and struggles. At that moment in time, I knew I was completely willing, I was desperate, but hadn't I been desperate before? Hadn't I tried to straighten up my life before? And it had never worked. It's funny how on my knees, in that chapel, in that moment, the powers of the enemy raised their ugly heads against me. They whispered lies and tried to discourage me. They told me it didn't work, He didn't work, He wasn't enough. But cue Grace, the angel God sent to pray with me. From a sobbing mess of a very broken young woman came these words: "I am willing now to surrender everything, but I am not sure I will be willing tomorrow." And then the words of truth Grace uttered chased all those whispers of the enemy back to hell. She said, "You will have to pick up your cross daily for the rest of your life and follow Him, but He will give you the strength."

What truth! What a powerful truth from the heart of our King. I wonder how many lies the devil tries to whisper to us over our lifetime? How many times has he tried to tell you that you are too messed up, that God isn't enough, that religion doesn't work? It's not about a religion, folks. It's about Jesus and the life and relationship He offers those who completely surrender to Him. He will give us His strength every day—every minute—to live a life honoring Him. We will indeed have to pick up our cross daily and choose to follow Him, but once we taste and see that the Lord is good, that cross becomes lighter and even a joy to bear. He is worthy.

That day, I knew what I needed to do. Realizing that the future direction of my life was dependent on my obedience was a game changer. I wish every day could be the same, that the new direction from the Creator would come to me on a daily basis. I would be lying if I told you it did. However, there are times when the Lord's voice is so completely clear that it is wonderfully scary.

Sometimes we may not want to go in the direction He is leading, but we should anyway. Sometimes we may not hear His direction as clearly as we would like, but keep listening. Sometimes we are afraid, things don't make sense, or we don't see how "that" can be a good thing. Let God be God, and allow Him to lead you. He knows best.

I have lived outside the United States for more than a decade. My desire has always been to bring glory to His name as I try to live a life obedient to the call. I have learned so much about God and myself. My need for a Savior never waivers, even if I do.

Thankfully it happens much less often, but I do hit seasons of being homesick for the United States. I miss family, friends, church, food, conveniences, holiday decorations, women's groups, and the language, just to name a few. My flesh cries out that we have only one life to live, and look at what I'm missing. That flesh of mine can be pretty blunt and relentless. It's a place in my soul where I hate to go. It's the place that says, "If only you (insert verb), *then* you will be happy, content." It's the place of looking inward, it's the place of believing lies, it's the place of idols; it is *not* a good place.

Then the Lord speaks, usually after I walk in obedience by feeding myself with His Word. This encounter should not be confused with the Lord showing up. He is always there. This message from the Lord is a product of obedience and desperation, of one of His children seeking Him with all their heart and in truth. Maybe you know what I mean.

Recently, the Lord used "our thing" and spoke to me two separate times. It makes me smile to think how much He loves me that He would honor my stubbornness and lay out a fleece—twice—for me. The first time He brought this particular direction to mind, I was reading in Deuteronomy 13. I was down in the dumps and honestly not even seeking the Lord to bring up my spirits but rather trying to be faithful in my daily reading. Deuteronomy 13 commands believers not to listen to those saying, "Let us go after other gods... and let us serve them" (Deut. 13:2 ESV). Rather, it tells believers, "You shall walk after the LORD your God and fear him and keep his commandments and obey his voice" (Deut. 13:4 ESV). After reading this, the Lord spoke in my spirit that I was being one of those naysayers, leading myself and my family away from our God with my attitude. However, as is usually the case with me, I allowed myself, even though I was convicted, to stay in that pit. The Lord knew I was still there, so He sent another word.

It came in the form of my Bible study, *Jesus the One and Only*, by Beth Moore. Gotta love Beth! She was talking about the name

Immanuel. It means *God with us.* It is a beautiful proper noun indicating who Jesus was and is. She explained that the Greek *Immanuel* is translated from the Hebrew *El* meaning *God*, and the rest of the word means *with us.* Therefore, *Immanuel* literally means *God with us.* What a sweet reminder! A story from Exodus 33 in the Old Testament was then pointed out to me—one very familiar to most of us. To fill you in, the Lord has just sent 10 plagues to Egypt, walked His people through the Passover of death, parted the Red Sea, destroyed their enemies, provided the Israelites with manna, and much more. But they stupidly built themselves a golden calf while their leader, Moses, was on Mount Sinai speaking to the God of creation on their behalf. The story still flabbergasts me.

Moses goes back to the mountain to try to make atonement for them (Exod. 32:30), and the Lord speaks to Moses:

> *"Depart, go up from here, you and the people whom you have brought up from the land of Egypt, to the land of which I swore. . . . I will send an angel before you and I will drive out [your enemies]. Go up to a land flowing with milk and honey; for I will not go up in your midst."*
>
> —Exod. 33:1–3 NASB

God is giving in to their cries and saying to go, and He will send an angel for protection and protect them from their enemies. He will give them what they want in the land where they want to be, but He will not go with them.

I was in that pit. I wanted my way. I could go back to America, a land I see flowing with milk and honey. I could have angel protection and even my salvation intact. But what if my God did not go with me? I think I would have to agree with Moses and say no thanks. I want to be exactly where my God is with me.

And that, my friends, changed my heart, mind, and attitude. With those simple words from God, the cloud was lifted, and for the time being, I found myself content being where my God was and where He wanted me to be.

This particular struggle or pull has continued to be a weapon for the enemy, and quite honestly, it probably will be until I reach my real home in heaven. I try to be open about the struggle but not whiney. It is important to keep your struggles in the open and in the light. I wonder what the enemy might use in your life to pull you away from contentment in the Lord. Identify it, and then fight against it.

There are many books and Bible studies written about hearing the voice of God, listening to the Holy Spirit, and discerning His will for your life. Read some of those if you want sound theological direction. However, I can testify that the Lord speaks to those who look to Him for answers. I am truly no one special apart from Jesus. Apart from Him, I would not live on the mission field. Apart from Jesus, I would not have given birth to my seventh child with my best friend since middle school—a child who has blessed our lives abundantly. Apart from Him, I certainly would not be writing these words. But because He lives in me, I can do all those things. He has a plan for your life, too, an amazing plan full of adventure and purpose. He has a plan to bring glory and renown to His name and His kingdom. He is also a good Father and wants to guide those who look to Him. "If you, then, though you are evil, know how to give good gifts to your children, how much more will your Father in heaven give good gifts to those who ask him!" (Matt. 7:11). Because I know this, I can testify that He will speak to you. He will lead you.

Remember the story from 1 Kings 19 about Elijah? In the story, a strong wind came, but God was not in the wind. Then an earthquake came, but again, God was not in the earthquake. After the earthquake, a fire came, but God was not in the fire. Finally, after the fire, there was a still, small voice, and—you've got it—God was in the still. Small. Voice.

We need to remember that if the world is always yelling loudly around us, we are going to have a difficult time hearing His voice.

We have to discipline ourselves to get away and listen. God uses very few avenues to speak to us. His Word trumps all. We must know it, study it, and live by it. However, God is not limited, and He uses sermons, music, other believers, even nonbelievers. He has spoken to me using all those avenues, even dreams, though we must be mature and knowledgeable disciples and weigh what we've heard against the truth of scripture. God's Word always stands, is never wrong, and never contradicts itself (Deut. 4:2; Prov. 30:6).

Surrendering our lives to the Lord Jesus will not just sometimes, but always, take us into hard places where we think we shouldn't be. I recently listened to a podcast that said something like this: The world we live in will always choose easy and make compromises, but sometimes God wants to strengthen our spiritual muscles, and that is not always fun. However, we can claim this promise:

> *Consider it pure joy, my brothers and sisters, whenever you face trials of many kinds, because you know that the testing of your faith produces perseverance. Let perseverance finish its work so that you may be mature and complete, not lacking anything.*
>
> —James 1:2–4

Let's be people who are not afraid of hard times. As you are walking through what Josh and I like to call the minefields of life, take heart that the Lord has a purpose for the struggle. Just as we work out to strengthen our physical bodies, the Lord works out our faith to strengthen us and prepare us for the next struggle. All the pain has a purpose. Don't be afraid. If God is in control, He is for us, and if He is for us, what can stand against us (Romans 8:31)? Let's be people who say with confidence, "Here am I. Send me!" (Isa. 6:8).

CHAPTER 5

God Can Use Anything: Surrendering Idols

Those who cling to worthless idols turn away from God's love for them.

—Jon. 2:8

God can use anything and everything to bring glory to Himself. He can use brokenness. He can use joy. He can use people, situations, songs, sermons, weaknesses, and strengths. He can use whatever talents He has given you to bring Himself glory, if you allow it. Even an old idol, an old identity, a stronghold that you have surrendered can be used by God.

I can testify to this. I have lived and watched the love of my life have an idol turn into an avenue to bring glory to his King. It all started at the age of six. He put on a pair of football pads and a helmet, and his destiny was set. There is something about a boy and a ball and the permission to hit someone as hard as they can. I will never understand this, but I am also not a male.

Josh's love for the sport continued to grow all through elementary school and later into middle school and high school. He was just a boy trying to have fun, pass each class in school, chase girls, drive his Bronco through the mud as often as possible, and play as hard as he could each Friday night under the lights. He was a typical American high school boy with not a care in the world—until his sophomore year of high school when he actually started to think about college.

No one in Josh's family had ever gone to college, so the thought never really occurred to him. It wasn't long before the scouts started to set their eyes on this six-foot-four defensive end. Midway through his junior year, he had made up his mind that he could do it. He would be able to graduate with enough credits to get into college and play ball. He had to complete night classes and take the ACT and SAT three times each, but he became eligible. Several colleges started looking at him, including a place that would later change our lives forever.

Memories of traveling on the weekends with Josh and his mom to check out several colleges during our senior year fondly replay in my mind. At that time, Josh and I were just friends, but we had a deep love for each other. He finally decided on a small, picturesque college surrounded by mountains in northern Greenville County in South Carolina. It was perfect for him. He thought being in the mountains was ideal and being at a small school would help him stay out of trouble. His high school football coach knew one of the coaches at the college, so it was an easy transition. We had no idea at the time what impact North Greenville College (it has since become a university) would have on our lives.

Choosing that school is truly a testimony of how God can direct our steps even before we know Him in any way. The motto of the school is "Where Christ Makes the Difference," and boy, did He ever make a difference in *our* lives.

Josh heard about Jesus at a tent crusade at the very beginning of his freshman year. Listening to him tell this story always makes my heart leap. It is another precious and dear memory that he can't tell without getting goose bumps all over his arms. I've heard him communicate it a few hundred times, but it never gets old watching him remember the moment he met Jesus for the first time. As I sit here, I am wondering if you have a story like the one I am about to tell you—a story of a dead man walking in sin becoming alive in the freedom of Christ. Do you know God loves you and has a plan for your life? He loves you so much that He sent His one and only Son, Jesus, to this earth to die as a sacrifice—a sacrifice that was enough to cover all your sins. As Josh's story also shows, it's not enough to ask Jesus to be your Savior. He wants to be your Lord. He wants you to surrender all aspects of your life to His lordship. After all, wouldn't you rather have the Creator of the world in the driver's seat of your life?

But let's get back to Josh's story. One of the requirements of athletes at that small school was to attend a tent crusade at the beginning of the school year. Josh sat so far in the back that he was actually outside the tent. He had no interest in being there; however, listening to the pastor speak, Josh became captivated by what he was saying. As the pastor recalled Jesus's parable about the wheat and the tares and heaven and hell (Matt. 13:24–30), Josh says he knew the man was speaking directly to him and that he was going straight to hell. He went forward that night and asked Jesus to be his Savior. He likes to say that he got his get-out-of-hell insurance that night. But a walk with Jesus? Making Him Lord of his life? Giving the reins of his decisions to another? He had no idea where to even begin.

Nothing much changed in Josh's life after that night except for one very important thing. He began to feel something he had never felt before. He began to feel a conviction for his sin. The feeling was strange at first; after all, he was just doing all the things he had always done, partying, having a good time, sleeping with his girlfriend. But this time, it felt different. And he hated it. He hated the feeling that came as he continued to live in the flesh. However, he wasn't willing or ready to hand over lordship of his life to God. Honestly, I don't think he even understood what that meant.

The only class he ever failed his entire life was chapel in his freshman year of college. And do you know why he failed? He didn't go. He hated the feeling of conviction. He would hear amazing speakers talk about sin, talk about grace, talk about surrendering, talk about Jesus, and he just ran. It would be months until he truly surrendered his life to the Lord, but I know from the day he received Jesus as his Savior that he was a child of God.

Maybe this is you. Maybe you have prayed a prayer and asked Jesus to be your Savior. Maybe you have realized there is really nothing you can do to be good enough. After all, you believe Jesus already paid your penalty for sin, so you truly opened your heart and gave Him a place in there, somewhere. But you still feel empty, alone. You question whether you really ever prayed the right prayer, and every time you get a chance, you say the prayer—one more time—just to make sure. I am thinking that many of you feel like that, and I am here to tell you there is more. There is so much more. You may have eternal life, but do you have abundant life? Are you excited about what God is doing in and through you? Do you see a difference in the way you live in your world? Around your kids? With your spouse?

You must give the Lord the reins, dear friend. Let Him take over. Surrender.

The love of our precious Jesus didn't give up on my stubborn man. He pursued and waited. He had a plan for Josh, just like He has a plan for you. Anyone who claims Jesus as their Lord and Savior can claim the promise that God has a plan for them. For many years, God's plan was for Josh to play football. Football got him through high school and gave him the chance to go to college. Football taught him life lessons about hard work, how to win with grace (is there such a thing?), teamwork, respect, and a myriad of other good attributes. He worked hard and often was able to bask in the benefits of his hard work.

But football did something else for Josh that wasn't so good. It defined him. He put all his identity into being a football player. Who was Josh Hepner? A dang good football player, that's who. Football became an idol in his life. It became more important than anything, any earthly relationship, and certainly any relationship with His heavenly Father.

Did you know that anything can become an idol? Anything that we elevate to the position that only God should have is an idol. I've had many idols over the course of my journey in life. Alcohol. Image. Marriage. Love. Entertainment (TV). Pills. Kids. To the world, some of these things seem good, and others seem bad. But I am here to tell you that anything we set above the Lord is harmful to our spiritual well-being. Anything in which we find ourselves placing our identity is fleeting. If I place all my hope in that man beside me and one day he is not there, then what? If I spend all my time and energy being supermom, what happens when it's time to send my children off to college? Who will I be in the wake of their departure? God is the only One who can fill that God-sized hole. He is the only One worthy. I must find my identity in Him; you must find your identity in Him.

God took football away from Josh. I can say that now because hindsight is 20/20. At the time, it just made sense. We had graduated from college and were doing all we could to keep our heads above water as we were juggling two children, a new marriage, a few jobs, church, and more. Josh had to make a decision about whether to pursue what every athlete, every little boy, dreams of—the top of the spectrum, the National Football League (NFL).

Could he have gone to the league? Maybe. He could have chosen the path of playing semipro and working his way up. He actually started playing a little semipro ball. He could have potentially sacrificed his family for this dream that lives in the heart of every little boy. However, he chose us. He says he hung up his pads and, in a way, gave up an identity that he'd had for so long. Looking back, I know it was the Lord. I know it was Jesus's will for Josh to choose the path he chose. I am so thankful that His plans are far greater than our own.

So as football was taken away, little did we know it was only taken away for a few seasons. God had other things to work into Josh's heart. He wanted to fill him with a new identity of being a surrendered follower of Christ. It took a few years of stepping away from the sport for Josh to realize the deep roots it had taken in his heart. Again, football was a great thing—not a bad thing—but it became the main thing, which should be a God thing.

Fast-forward five years. We had finally graduated from college, added our daughters Abigail and Darcie to the family, bought a house, sold the house and everything else we owned, and committed our lives to international missions. Goodness! It makes me tired just writing all of that.

We were finally ready to take that leap of faith, sort of. I think I will forever be grateful for the naivety that existed in our minds and hearts at that time. At that point, we needed to make a decision about *where* we were going. Kind of a big one, yeah? Some people are called to a people group, a country, or even a continent. We were really completely open with a here-am-I-send-me attitude.

The day finally arrived for our conference with the sending agency that we love and are so grateful for. The conference was a time where we could look through books of available jobs all over the world. They were divided into continents, religions, people groups, and job categories. Since we did not have a people group or a place in mind, we went for the job categories. We had both earned a bachelor's degree in education, so we naturally thought we could teach somewhere. It only made sense to begin our search there. We quickly found a great job request for a teacher at an international school in Sri Lanka. It sounded promising, so we spoke with the representative at the conference who was representing South Asia. Out of more than 5,000 people in the company, would you believe that the couple representing that part of the world wrote the very job request we were considering? Josh and I looked at each other with wonder in our eyes at how the Lord works. We sat down and had a two-hour talk with this amazing couple. We thought they were great, we thought the job sounded promising, and we couldn't possibly deny the Lord's hand in the process of orchestrating this meeting with our potential future supervisors. But we got up from the table hand in hand, looked at each other, and almost simultaneously said, "That's *not* it." To this day, it still surprises us how much we were on the same page. We just knew deep down inside that this was not a fit for us.

Have you ever had a moment like that? It's something that looks good, a decision that makes sense, but you just know you are not supposed to do it? That, my friend, is the Holy Spirit working in us. Sometimes things may look good and may even be good, but maybe they are not the best for us. God always wants what is best for us. It's in the surrender that we realize how trustworthy He is.

Josh and I were both a little discouraged having to go back to the books to begin looking for jobs again. We had exhausted our efforts with the teaching jobs. I remember sitting in the lobby of this big building feeling kind of lost when Josh said, "Let's look at sports jobs." Okay, why not? I thought. Although anyone who knows me would not classify me as the sporty type; my man was all about that. As we began looking through a list, it was not long until we came across a job request for an American football player and coach for a small country in the Balkans.

Josh saw football, and I saw Europe. Our excitement grew as we spoke to the European representative who then gave us the phone and told us to call our future supervisors. Josh asked questions about the job—the whos, the whats, the whens, and the wheres involving football. My questions were more along the lines of safety, weather, and schooling options. We both had our priorities straight, of course. We took the job and committed to serving a two-year term.

That night we lay in bed and talked for hours, in awe of how the Lord could be giving football back to Josh. And that He did. Boy, has He used it for His glory. As I write this, we have lived there for more than 10 years. The Lord has allowed Josh to both play and now coach over the past decade. He has met countless men and has been able to encourage them on and off the field. He has coached for two teams, traveled all over Europe with the National Team, helped grow the football program to include flag teams, youth, junior, senior, and even a women's league, and has earned the respect of every football club in the country. Football has morphed into an identity for our family to have legitimacy in a country that frowns on change and outsiders. With our identity fully planted in Jesus and our job title planted in football, our hearts remained anchored in finding fulfillment in Him and fun in football. With the help of many national partners and the power of God, we have been part of planting a church in two cities and have raised our children there. And to this day, when people ask how we ended up living there, we always say God—and football.

> *Each of you should use whatever gift you have received to serve others, as faithful stewards of God's grace in its various forms.*
>
> —1 Pet. 4:10

CHAPTER 6

As a Servant of the King: Surrendering Desires

Delight yourself in the LORD, and he will give you the desires of your heart.

—Ps. 37:4 ESV

S ome days, I feel like I could write an entire book on the subject of surrendering your desires. But what about the scriptures that tell us to delight in the Lord and He will give us the desires of our heart? That is true, right?

Absolutely. It's in scripture, so it must be true. Unfortunately, this verse is often taken out of context. I do not think God called us to an easy life, which is what our flesh wants, or a life of luxury and ease. He does tell us we can have life and truly live that life to the fullest (John 10:10). So what about getting the desires of our heart?

To live by that verse, we have to learn to live *both* parts of the verse—the "delight yourself in the Lord" part and "the desires of your heart" part. It is when we try to live out the latter without the previous that things get out of whack.

I wish I could say that I delight in the Lord all the time, but that would be a lie. Let's talk about this in terms of parenthood for a little ˙bit.

We all have goals for our children. We want the very best for them. We want them to have good grades, solid friends, and enduring faith in the Lord. We want them to become productive citizens who contribute to their generation. My constant prayer for my children is that they will change their generation by honoring God and making His Kingdom famous here on earth as in heaven. Yes, Lord Jesus, please! But the journey to become such amazing people takes some shepherding, some parenting, that they are not always thrilled to receive. Who likes to be disciplined? Who likes to be changed into something that is against our flesh?

The Lord must have access to our hearts, and we must desire Him; but it might not always be fun. We must learn hard lessons like the obedience that has to take place and will cause us pain. But I have come to learn that we serve a loving Father who wants nothing but the very best for each of His children.

I know that my own children first need to begin to sleep through the night. What newborn baby likes that? Then they need to learn to go to the potty on their own—one of my least favorite things to teach my children. Then we need to tackle skills such as learning to tie shoes, ride a bike, and read a book. What do all those skills take? Practice. And who is the one to remind them to practice? Sometimes life will be that teacher—they will have to go to the bathroom at some point and will probably want to tie those shoes on their own so they can hurry out the door. Sometimes they really do have a drive to learn. Those are the easy tasks we as parents get to do—the times often documented on video or film such as first steps, first bike rides, first time down the waterslide, and first time down the side of a mountain on that new sled. Children have an internal desire to achieve those goals, and it is a pleasure to teach them. It is a joy to parents to teach them those lessons.

I think there are some lessons the Lord allows life to teach us, such as hard work helps us get good paychecks, determination helps us get through school, and laughter helps our hearts feel light. Of course, His hands are in it all, but just living life teaches us these things. Likewise, there are times when the Lord teaches us directly and we remain teachable. We are His delight; we want to learn. I can think of times when I was obedient to meet a need, speak an encouraging word, or offer forgiveness, and that is where I felt His delight.

Parents must also teach lessons that are not fun. Disciplines must be learned for our children to live up to their full potential, and those take practice. One of the first lessons I usually have to battle over with my children is cleaning their room. It may be fun at first to help Mom and make her happy, but then it gets old, and they don't want to do it. So we have to remind them, gently at first. Then if they still don't obey, consequences may be in order. The habit must be formed. Teaching children how to read is another. Lord knows this one stresses me out. I am halfway there. I've taught four children, just three more to go. Hurry and come back, Jesus.

Teaching children how to read takes patience, repetition, patience, consistency, patience, practice, and did I mention patience? Whew! Again, at first it is fun to learn letters and even read those first few words. But after that, well, I liken it to pulling teeth. I have an avid reader. Abigail will read anything that stays still long enough. She loves it. Reading is her happy place, but it did not start off that way. I have another daughter, Darcie, who has dyslexia. Teaching her to read, well, let's just say that the Lord grew my patience in ways I did not believe possible. My sweet girl is amazing, and she achieved her goal, but reading did not come easily—for either of us.

Aren't we a lot like children when it comes to learning to delight ourselves in the Lord? Some things are fun, easy, and exciting. We may enjoy entering into His presence through worship. Just like riding that bike, we need no reminding. We tried it once, and it was amazing. We will do it again. Or maybe it's like receiving God's grace and forgiveness. That feels good, and just like that waterslide we got brave enough to try, even though it felt scary at first, it turned out to be the best, and we don't have to be reminded to do it over and over again.

Other lessons may be like learning to read, and they require practice. They need discipline. They may be things like maintaining a quiet time and a vibrant prayer life. We know we need to learn how to read; it's vital to becoming an integral part of a productive society. But it's hard, and it takes practice. The same idea applies to maintaining a quiet time. Some days it feels better to stay in bed. Sometimes it just seems too confusing. The adversary lies to us that it's not making a difference. But the Father reminds us to practice, to stick with it. It will be worth it and will produce fruit that will lead us to becoming a productive member of His Kingdom.

Then we have the matter of obedience, of surrender to what the Lord has for our lives, our days, and even each hour. Does He *really* want us to give that much money? Is He *really* asking me to share the gospel with that person? Do I *really* need to say I'm sorry? Obedience. Surrender. A Sunday school teacher taught me an illustration years ago. When making a decision, think of a see-saw with God on one side and you on the other. Weigh the decision and ask yourself if taking action is exalting yourself or lifting up the Lord. If God is lifted, then you, my friend, are going to be lower than He is. "He must become greater; I must become less" (John 3:30).

For the past 18 years, my family, the Hepners, have had this conversation at least once a week, if not several times a day. Josh or I will ask the kids, "How do we obey?" They reply, "All the way, right away, and with a joyful heart." For the task of cleaning their bedroom, this would look like cleaning it completely the way Mom likes it (all the way), the moment they are asked (right away), and without complaining, huffing, or back talking (with a joyful heart). I heard this piece of wisdom many years ago from an author named Ginger Plowman, and I loved it. If we can teach our children to obey us this way, then by God's grace, they will obey Him the same way as adults. When God asks something of them, I pray with all my being that they will obey Him, all the way, right away, and with a joyful heart. I also pray that I will live that example for them as they watch the way I obey my heavenly Father.

I've learned recently that one of my spiritual gifts—my top one, in fact—is discernment. This basically means that God has given me a natural ability to be able to discern good and evil in people, in situations, and in decisions. I wish I always did this perfectly; ask my husband, and he will attest that I do not. However, sometimes I do, and it's spot on. I really need to explore this aspect of myself a little more.

My natural tendency is to run away quickly from any type of spiritual warfare. I know it exists, but I do not like to stay there long. I have a weakness when it comes to fear, but I am learning that fear is not of the Lord, which means it is from the devil and therefore has no place in my life. Have I mentioned that I am a major work in progress? It makes me think of Ruth Graham's headstone, which says, "End of Construction—Thank you for your patience." What a beautiful legacy and a poignant truth that punched me in the gut when I read it. We are ever-evolving works of the Father, clay in the Potter's hands (Isa. 64:8).

There was once a woman in our lives who was, well, different—eccentric. She was in her 40s and had been coming to our newly formed

Bible study that met in our home. She was a beautiful woman who, like most Balkan women, dressed to impress. We would often laugh that her presence at our house group would almost always ensure the presence of a few of Josh's football players. She wore short skirts and low-cut (sometimes see-through) shirts. I don't remember how we met her, but I do remember that she was into everything. Like many people we meet who claim to be spiritual, she liked dabbling in Tarot cards, reading the leftover grounds in her coffee, and lighting candles. Then she decided to try out an American "sect" who loved Jesus.

Our home group met on Sunday nights, and on this particular evening, she asked Josh for a ride home. She lived in a village outside of town, not too far away but not too close, either. Josh and I have had a rule in our marriage for years that we do not ride alone in a car with members of the opposite sex. This is to protect both us and our integrity as it removes the chance of rumors starting. Anyway, that meant I had the privilege on this particular night of driving this woman home.

The ride there was uneventful, but when we arrived in the village and it was time for her to get out of my car, she had a question. It was dark, y'all—very dark—other than the lights from my own car. I looked over into her very dark brown eyes to hear the question: "Do you believe you can be possessed by the devil?" *Everything* in me was on high alert. Sirens were going off in my brain, the hair on my head stood up, chill bumps rose on my arms, my breathing quickened, and my heart stood still. Immediately, my mouth opened without my brain telling it what to say, and out came, "In the name of Jesus Christ, I am sealed!" What? Where did that truth even come from? The Holy Spirit, of course. He gives us words when we have none. I was terrified. Remember, I don't do that spiritual warfare stuff. It scares me. But here I was in the middle of this unseen war; however, I was on the winning side.

This thought came to me while I was writing this book. In the house where our home group met, I used to have horrifying dreams.

There was one I had several times. I am not talking about your run-of-the-mill dream. I am talking about a spiritual-warfare-battle type of dream, one that has a physical presence of something dark. This particular reoccurring dream was of a woman, a snakelike woman with long, red fingernails who would slither from a distance and come close to my face. I have wondered if there is a connection. Was this woman a conduit of an unwelcome spirit? We need to be diligent to pray over our homes after people have come in who are not sealed in Christ. I am not saying you should avoid inviting people in, but by all means, show them Christ's love and be sure to pray over your home once they leave.

In the car that night, I gathered my thoughts and explained to her that once Jesus comes into your heart, you are a sealed being, and that while evil spirits and the devil can mess with you, nothing can possess you other than His precious Holy Spirit (Eph. 1:13). I pray that she heard my words, that the Lord used them. But really, I just wanted her out of my car. Once she left, the Lord and I had a little talk that went something like this: *Lord, I am done! Take this woman out of my life. She is scary and immodest, and I don't love her. Why do you have her in my life? I will talk with Ivana tomorrow, share with Vanja this week, but take this woman out of my life.*

I was begging, feeling completely desperate, even afraid, and not wanting to have to deal with her in any way ever again. I have to admit that I was even angry. Almost immediately, in the middle of my begging, a sermon came to mind that I had recently heard. The pastor was making the point of being a servant to a king. He said that if we are true, loyal, and good servants, we do not go before our King bargaining. We don't need to say if You do this, or this, or that, then I will serve You, but rather, we lay prostrate before our King and say, "Here am I; use me as You see fit."

I entered the house in a full-on ugly cry. Josh had to be scared to death as it took me several minutes to explain to him what the Lord had just spoken to my heart. Jesus was asking me to surrender my desires for His desires. His heart is for the lost, and while it can be hard for my flesh to love them, it is not hard for our God. Although I did not understand the plan, I understood my place. I am a servant to the King, and He is the One I obey.

I believe the key to having the King meet the desires of your heart is to delight in Him. Delight in His love, mercy, and grace, but also learn to find delight in His justice and discipline. Trust His heart and His plan, even when it doesn't make sense or when it seems scary. It wasn't long after that car ride that the lady stopped coming to our house church. I have not seen her in more than eight years. I pray for her on occasion and truly hope that she listened to His voice calling her into a saving relationship with Him, but I don't know that for sure, and I probably won't on this side of heaven. Nonetheless, I am thankful for her and for the Lord using her to teach me a lesson on surrendering my desires to Him.

I have no idea what the Lord is asking of you. Maybe He wants you to speak truth into someone who is very difficult. He will give you the words to say. Obey Him. Maybe He wants you to write a letter and seek reconciliation with someone who has wronged you. Forgiveness may equal freedom for you. Maybe He wants you to be honest about that secret sin that tortures you in the night. Find someone you can trust and confess to them; bring it into the light. There is healing and freedom in Christ. Maybe He wants you to surrender to a call on your life for the purposes of His Kingdom. Take the step and get out of the boat. People will question you and wonder if you are crazy, but remember, as a believer in Jesus Christ, your loyalties belong with the King. Obey Him.

CHAPTER 7

He Makes It Okay with Your Heart: Surrendering Family

Therefore, I urge you, brothers and sisters, in view of God's mercy, to offer your bodies as a living sacrifice, holy and pleasing to God—this is your true and proper worship.

—Rom. 12:1

Leaving the comfort of the ideal life we had made was the furthest thing from my mind. We had worked so hard with various goals in sight to finish college, get jobs, pay off debt, buy a house, get plugged into a good church. Check, check, check. We did it all. We were finally there. I don't know what I expected or wanted after that. Just to live a fulfilling life? To be normal? To have family get-togethers, birthday parties, and soccer games? To watch the kids grow up and flourish in all they were involved in, especially in the Lord? What was the idol? The beautiful draw? I guess it was to give them everything I had ever wanted—a place in this world to call my own, their own, a safe and healthy environment. Maybe it was my house on the hill that I would live in all my life with all my babies, a place for them to forever call home. Even as I write this, something inside me yearns for that. But a surrendered life calls us to something much greater than that. A surrendered life lays down those idols in an effort to pursue the One who is worthy.

When Josh came home talking about missions, I was dumbfounded. *Seriously? You want to what? Sell everything we have worked for and move to who knows where? With my children? What about our families? What about our jobs? What about...?* I was a mess. Nevertheless, the God of my heart began pursuing me ever so gently. I often say that Josh is the gas, and I am the brake. While I am usually pretty easygoing, this was one idea I was *slamming* the brakes on. No way, nohow!

As I have already mentioned, the Lord's gentle whisper turned into a constant chatter. It got to the point that it was all I could think about. I grieved, I worried, and I dwelt on all the things I thought I knew about being a cross-cultural minister. Looking back, I knew absolutely nothing, and part of me is grateful for that naivety. I liken it in my mind to the innocence of a newly married couple. Have you ever gone to a wedding and looked at the sweet couple and thought to yourself, "They have no idea!"

Have you ever felt the Lord calling you to something and decided to put up a fight? Maybe you rationalized in your mind that you heard wrong, that you didn't really need to say sorry, or that it wasn't necessary to be kind to your grumpy boss. Maybe you just get really busy with this or that and don't make time to be obedient. Maybe you are terrified to journey into the deeper faith you know He is calling you to, so you just pretend, run scared, or decide it's better to not get too serious about this Jesus stuff. I've done them all, but let me tell you, He is worth it, sweet friend. Jesus is worth all the sacrifice. He is worth all the persecution. He is worth everything you will be asked to lay down for His name. Walking the fence or lukewarm, not-too-deep Christianity is what will get you in trouble. It makes us numb to His voice. It opens the door wide for the schemes of the enemy. It prevents us from being the person He wants us to become.

I want to be used for His glory. I want people to remember me as a woman who loved Jesus and her man and her babies like a crazy person. Life is better with Jesus. Things stay in focus, and priorities stay in line. Without Jesus, life is confusing, without purpose, and totally about self. Do you want to be remembered as a lost soul who floundered through life searching for purpose, loving when it was convenient, and living for yourself? Or would you like your children and grandchildren to remember you as someone sold out to living a surrendered life, a life with purpose to love and laugh and forgive and die to self, all in an effort to bring glory to the Creator of the world? Yep, that one. Pick Him!

Recently, while completing a Bible study, I read something that stuck with me. It posed a similar question: Do you want to be a woman who just carries a Bible around under her arm, or do you want to be a woman who knows and understands that playbook of life and lives by it? We make it so complicated sometimes. *The Bible is so hard to understand, it's so dated, blah, blah, blah.* Stick with what you know, ladies. We can all understand "Love the LORD your God with all your heart and with all your soul and with all your strength" (Deut. 6:5). That's easy to understand, right? Well, do it! Show love to this lost and dying world. We all can also understand this:

> *Do not be anxious about anything, but in every situation, by prayer and petition, with thanksgiving, present your requests to God. And the peace of God, which transcends all understanding, will guard your hearts and your minds in Christ Jesus.*
>
> —Phil. 4:6–7

There you have it. Stop worrying, and start praying. I am sure I could think of many other biblical references that are neither physics nor too complicated. I believe if we as a body would start actually living by what we know to be right, we could change the world. Stick with the basics.

Let's get back to the whisper that turned into chatter that turned into a loud voice. By the time we sold it all, packed up what was left, gave those heart-wrenching, see-ya-later hugs, and boarded that plane, I seemed to be a surrendered servant. The problem that often arises is in the heart attitude of my obedience. Begrudgingly surrendering is quite different from joyfully surrendering. This is something I am still working through.

As we were surrendering to the process of moving overseas and praying about where in the world God would lead us, I kept bringing up to Josh my worries or attitudes about the various choices. I would often say things like, "Okay, let's go, just not to a place where there is a threat to our safety, or where I have to worry about bugs killing my children, or where it is always freezing cold." Frustrated, Josh would tell me to stop putting stipulations on God, and I would walk away with my tail tucked and my mouth shut. So although I did not voice my list, I was constantly adding bullet points.

He knows us so well, our Father—and He knew all about my list. He created us from the dust of the ground and breathed life into us. He knows what we like to eat, what we feel most comfortable wearing. He created in us our desires and talents. He also knows our fears and concerns. One of my favorite verses is Jeremiah 29:11, which says, "'For I know the plans I have for you,' declares the LORD, 'plans to prosper you and not to harm you, plans to give you hope and a future.'" God has a plan for each of us. It is only when we live a life surrendered to Him that we are able to bask in His prosperity, in His future, in His hope. Again, He is worth it, dear friend.

So many times since moving overseas, I have seen how my sweet Jesus has taken care of me and guided my steps. On our first trip back home, the message the Lord laid on my heart to share with American churches was this: "Whatever God calls you to do, He makes it okay with your heart." It will forever be one of the sweetest lessons the Lord has allowed me to learn. But do you know what I had to do to be able to learn that lesson? Obey.

One particular morning, I was standing in our kitchen overseas during a moment that happened to be quiet. The kids were preoccupied in another room, Josh was out and about, and I was alone in the kitchen, being a mom. But I wasn't alone for long because on this particular morning, the Lord decided to join me.

As I stood there, a sunbeam shone through the window, and the lover of my soul tapped me on the shoulder and spoke to my heart. "Hey, Kristen, remember that list? How'd I do?" And then it came— peace. Undeniable peace. I was right where I was supposed to be. Through difficulties and hard days, He had heard my requests and was oh so faithful with where He had placed our family. We were living in a safe place that cherished families and children above all else. There were no bugs, that I knew of, that could kill my children. It got cold, but not to the point that my skin would freeze if the wind touched it. Over the past decade, there have been countless times when we have seen how this country suits our personalities in ways that only the Lord could design. He is ever so faithful, sweet friend. Instead of honoring my list of stipulations, He changed this stubborn heart to match His will.

Surrendering my life was hard, but surrendering the lives of my children continues to be a challenge. About six months into living in our new country, I was up in the attic hanging clothes. Yes, in the attic. It was a really neat spot in our first home that had unfinished concrete floors, cobweb-covered wooden beams that held up the roof's infamous European ceramic red tiles, several clotheslines, and a tiny door that opened from the bathroom and housed my washing machine. Great little setup. I was there hanging clothes to dry when I heard neighborhood kids using what little English they had to taunt my children. "What is your name? What is your name?" over and over again. I knew that my two oldest, ages six and four at the time, were outside playing. I also knew that these neighborhood kids were much older and much louder than my sweet babies. "What is your name? What is your name?" My mama bear began to awaken. I tried to go about my business, but after a few minutes, my inner voice was roaring in a full growl. I ran down the stairs and out the back door.

"Dayne! Abigail!" I yelled. "It's time to come inside."

How dare these kids talk to my babies like that! Don't they see they are little? Talk to me all you want, make fun of me, but leave my children alone! I fumed inwardly.

I had made my way out the back door and was standing on the porch when Dayne, the older of the two, ran around the corner of the house—alone.

"Where's your sister?" I demanded in a voice that was probably too loud.

"I don't know, Mom," he replied, clearly aggravated that I was making him come inside.

Stomping down the stairs, I flew around the corner of the house. The scene before me still makes me smile and humbles me to my knees. My beautiful, blond-haired baby was practically glowing in the sunshine as she handed a bright, yellow dandelion through the fence to the ringleader of the neighborhood crowd. It was God's whisper to me that my children were going to be just fine. Regardless of how I felt, they felt at home and at peace.

While seasons do come when I mourn for them missing family events, seeing friends at church, playing football for their schools, attending prom, and all the other things we as mothers look forward to watching our children do, I have come to realize that this—our life, our call—was a call for them, too. They are little ministers. God knew at the beginning of time the plan He was writing for them, which included growing up overseas. I can't wait to see how God is going to use them as they grow up. Our prayer has always been for our children to radically change their generation for the

Kingdom. I pray that they, too, will learn to surrender their entire lives to the Master's plan.

The impact our family has made on the communities where we have lived may never be known this side of heaven, but I will tell you that my children have grown into young people who know how to serve. They have poured out their lives in their schools and in our churches. They have served countless guests in our home. They have lived a missional life and have sacrificed so much, more than they even understand. However, if you were to ask any of them whether they would trade our life for another, that we should have made a different decision and chosen not to move overseas but rather live the normal American life, they would all say, "No way!" Every. Single. One. While extremely hard and often lonely times have been their lot, they have been able to experience different cultures and have been at the front lines of a spiritual battle. They have learned how to speak another language and have endured countless times of teasing for their accents. They have appreciated the delicacies of very different cuisines and have missed cold cereal and processed fast foods. They have learned how to sing to Jesus in another language while deeply longing to connect to God in English. They have had to serve in church rather than be served. They have had to miss family and holidays and birthdays while teaching others what it means to celebrate as Americans. Was it hard for this mama to do that to them? Absolutely! However, the One who loves them even more than I could ever think or imagine planned it all before the beginning of time.

To say I am proud of Dayne, Abigail, Darcie, Josiah, Jase, Emma, and Levi is an understatement. I am in awe of them. They inspire me every day to love more deeply, serve with more intensity, and choose more joy than I ever thought possible. While my human heart wanted to protect them from so much, the Lord gave me enough strength to surrender them to His will, and they are incredible humans because of Him.

CHAPTER 8

Reconfirmation of the Call: Surrendering Again and Again

But because of his great love for us, God, who is rich in mercy, made us alive with Christ even when we were dead in transgressions—it is by grace you have been saved. And God raised us up with Christ and seated us with him in the heavenly realms in Christ Jesus, in order that in the coming ages he might show the incomparable riches of his grace, expressed in his kindness to us in Christ Jesus. For it is by grace you have been saved, through faith—and this is not from yourselves, it is the gift of God.

—Eph. 2:4–8

I had a spiritual attack today, though not the kind in which you feel an evil presence. I've had those, too, but this one was just a sort of cloud over my head. I didn't call it that to begin with; I kind of went with it. It started with just a thought—a good thought, actually. We were preparing to leave for five months in the States, and the amount of preparation on both ends was enough to give anyone a mild panic attack. Housing, transportation, logistics, cell phones, continuation of ministry, speaking at churches, time with family—the list goes on and on. However, my thoughts were not swirling around those worries; instead, I was thinking how much I enjoyed life in America, how everything was easier there, how I'd wake up each day excited about what the day would hold, how people appreciated my presence and I appreciated theirs. Truth? Yes. From the Lord? Debatable.

I have been here before. You see, for things to look so wonderful in America makes everything anywhere else pale in comparison. Those thoughts don't lead me to a good place but to a place of discontentment and disobedience.

The enemy is sly. He knows how to plant enticing thoughts that don't really seem sinful to begin with but can quickly turn into disgruntlement, dissatisfaction, and sin. Any time we try to take the reins, we pick up our own agenda, which consequently makes us drop God's agenda and even His will. Haven't we walked with Him long enough to truly believe that His way is best? Yet we can still find ourselves believing lies and allowing discontentment to take root.

How many of us daydream our way into the sin of discontentment? Don't get me wrong; dreaming is a healthy habit with excellent benefits. Setting goals and achieving dreams give us perseverance and purpose and make us productive human beings. However, a fine line exists that, when crossed, can turn those pursuits into idols. Having a glass-half-empty attitude and always thinking the grass is greener on the other side is ultimately telling God what He's given is not enough. We have to train our hearts and minds to be like Paul, to find contentment in *all* things (Phil. 4:10–13).

Let me summarize what Paul said in this passage. I have learned to be content in any circumstance. I've been in need, and I've had everything I wanted. I have learned the secret, people, even if I am hungry or living with a need. And just when we all say something like, "Great, Paul! Good for you! Could you please share with us what it is that leads to that contentment?" he gives us the answer that many of us have heard many times: "I can do all this through him who gives me strength" (Phil 4:13). But really, deep down, we already knew that, didn't we? Jesus! Jesus is the answer. Jesus is the cure.

A few years ago, I was in a pit due to a series of days and months dwelling on thoughts like this. I was in a place of discontentment, wanting and demanding change, arguing with God that I had already given Him a decade. I asked Him if that wasn't enough already. I wanted to give up on everything—my ministry, my marriage, pretending I had it all together, the struggle of trying so hard. Have you ever been there? Have you ever reached rock bottom, as some say? Have you experienced a sense of defeat when you absolutely cannot go on? You are unable to even think clearly about your situation, even if you try. In your heart of hearts, you are done. Done! Completely done!

I was done. I don't think I can overemphasize how low I was. We all have our breaking points, I suppose, especially if we are living a life wearing masks. If we are not honest with ourselves, others, and even God, we are wearing a mask. If we absolutely convince ourselves that the fault lies solely in ourselves, we are living a lie. I had gotten so good at it that I could use scripture against myself. I could beat myself up, if you will, with all the reasons I was selfish and needed to suck it up.

Up to that point in my life, I had learned to cope with strong emotions by stuffing them down or pretending, by doing my best to talk myself out of the emotions I was feeling. For those of you who can relate, that is *not* a healthy way to live. If you haven't already, you will reach the end of your rope. Find someone to talk to before that happens, someone who can help you see the error of your ways, and learn a different way to deal with your emotions. I think many people live like this. They wrongly think this is the way God intended things to be, but it's not. He wants you to live in a place of authenticity, to be your genuine self. He wants you to be the way He made you, not the way you perceive you *should* be or the way anyone else would like you to be. He wants you to be true to yourself. You are fearfully and wonderfully made (Ps. 139:14). You are worth it. You are enough.

Many things were happening on many levels that brought me to this breaking point. Let's start with the obvious. We had moved to a new city after living in our Balkan hometown for seven years. I thought the move was relatively easy, and we really felt the Lord's hand on the actual decision to move. The reality proved more difficult. Within the first two months of arriving in our new city, I was pregnant with our sixth child, Emma. We were excited about the news and had anticipated this little life. What I did not anticipate was the lack of energy and enthusiasm that would accompany the pregnancy. You see, I had yet to make many friends in this new city, and I needed friends. To make friends, you have to put yourself out there and try to make friends, but I had no *try* in me. I was mothering five children who had also just moved to a new city, and I was growing a sixth. That is just one piece of this woe-is-me frame of mind I was in, but it was a big piece.

Josh and I were also not getting along well, mainly due to a lack of communication about almost everything. He, too, was trying to figure out the new normal in our new environment. He had a ton of pressure coming down on him from all directions, so I wanted to be his "easy." I put on a mask that all was well with me, thinking it would be selfish of me to bring him into my crazy struggle. That was my default coping method, and it had worked for years. I had learned to easily self-talk my way out of pretty much any feeling or emotion, all the while convincing myself that it didn't exist. I never listened to myself regarding my own needs. After all, that would be selfish, right?

I wish I could say that I realized on my own that the pretending wasn't going to work, that one day I would have an epiphany that I was a really broken and confused person who needed to do a lot of work on herself. But I didn't. As a matter of fact, it took me months of counseling and soul searching to finally see that the problem existed within me. I was absolutely certain nothing in the world was wrong with the way I was coping by pretending. I was also completely convinced that the source of my dissatisfaction was coming from everyone around me. Doesn't the Lord warn us of this?

> *How can you say to your brother, "Let me take the speck out of your eye," when all the time there is a plank in your own eye? You hypocrite, first take the plank out of your own eye, and then you will see clearly to remove the speck from your brother's eye.*
>
> —Matt. 7:4–5

Yet the problem remained. I legitimately did not see my own folly.

My eyes weren't opened until I hit a brick wall, and pretending became impossible in the destruction that came in the aftermath. Something in me snapped and broke; the mask fell off, and no amount of effort could put it back on. However, though it was ugly and messy and even scary, finally being honest about my feelings was the most liberating thing I had ever done. I was out in the open; the cat was out of the bag. Kristen was done pretending that all was right with her world when it wasn't.

Believe me when I say that I remember exactly where I was sitting when I slammed into that wall and broke. My sweet husband was the receiver of this flood of emotion. Poor guy! He had to have been terrified when his so well-put-together wife completely lost it. In reality, though, I think he would say that he knew it was coming and even welcomed the crash. We both knew something needed to change.

Now that I look back on it all, I suppose my spiritual life had become fake. I was obedient in going through the motions. I was reading the Word and praying, sometimes. I was sharing the gospel with the lost around me. I was supposed to be proclaiming the good news as a Christian, but do you know what? We are all just broken people trying our best to figure out how in the world to walk through this life.

When it all came flooding out, my solution was to return to the States. Living overseas made everything too difficult, I reasoned. I finally confessed out loud that life was too hard. Homeschooling was hard. Kids were hard. Marriage was hard. The language was hard. Ministry was hard. It was *all* hard! I was done! And as far as I was concerned, we were moving back to America—signed, sealed, and delivered. The Hepners were done!

Thankfully, my husband was kind and patient in that moment of my being done. He was wise enough to validate my feelings that life was hard. He was also wise enough to bring God into the moment. I wasn't even pretending that I wanted God in that moment, but I agreed to pray with Josh. Actually, the prayer didn't change much. I was still ready to pack our bags and board a plane, but Josh asked if he could fast and pray for three days over the situation. I had no problem with that. He could fast and pray all he wanted, but I had no intention of joining him because I had already decided that I knew God would not change my heart. The hurts were too deep. But that turned out okay, too, because God had a plan. No hurt is too deep or too wide for the love of Christ.

I don't remember much about the next three days. I am sure I went through the motions of seeking the Lord, but my mind was made up, so my seeking was pointless. Do you ever find yourself there, where you know what *you* want but you pray anyway, trying your best to get the Lord to agree with you? Yeah, well, that's where I was. I was praying, all right. I was praying that the Lord would open Josh's eyes to see how miserable his wife was and to take her side, just this one time. Praise the Lord, I married a man who seeks God's will first, and I serve a God who wants our very best.

It was on the third day that the first phone call came. It was our current landlord's wife. We knew that her husband, Milan, had been sick with cancer and didn't have much time left on this earth. His precious wife was calling to ask Josh and our ministry partner, James, to come and pray over her husband since they knew we were a praying people.

Josh and James quickly went to Milan's bedside and prayed with him. They shared once again the free gift that Jesus offers to all people through His death on the cross. We don't know if Milan understood enough to be ushered into the kingdom of heaven a few days later, but we do know what a beautiful honor it was to be included in this monumental event in the lives of Milan and his family. It was humbling. We were grateful for the opportunity. God was using us. My heart was softening. I knew the Lord was at work in this. Something was stirring in my heart and in the heavenlies, which I never thought possible.

Later that evening, we received a phone call from a former landlord's grown daughter. Our relationship was a bit different with this family, as we had known them for years. They were very near and dear to our hearts. We had celebrated birthdays, Thanksgivings, Christmases, and other holidays with their precious family for years. The daughter called to let us know her father had been in a very serious car accident. She asked us to pray. She, too, knew that we prayed. Praise the Lord, Milanko survived the crash as well as several surgeries. He is doing well today, enjoying life and his grandchildren. The journey to health was not at all easy for him, but the Lord sustained his body and gave him resolve.

The weight of the second phone call was almost crushing to me. Two phone calls, two landlords, two deep needs involving the patriarchs of these families. The "coincidence" of it all still makes me stop in my tracks and take a deep breath. We all know good and well that there is no such thing as a coincidence. There is, however, an amazing God who sometimes awakens us and opens our eyes to see what *He* is doing all the time, all around us. God made it abundantly clear that we were making a difference *right where we were.* While there were thousands of other nationals those hurting families could have called, they called us. God was using us. It suddenly didn't matter how much I thought our return to America would make me happy again and make all my dreams come true. My view suddenly went from looking inward to looking outside of myself. Perspective—we need to constantly pray for a God's-eye view.

And just like that, the idol of returning to America was crushed. Josh's prayer and fasting had yielded fruit. God had my attention, and my heart was inclined once again to follow Him in obedience. I hurried to our love-note board to record the event. It's a place where we write sweet nothings to each other, record the dates of our babies' births, and collect inspiring quotes and scripture. That day, I wrote, "God confirmed our call. We are staying here!" I snapped a picture of my scribblings and sent it to Josh who, with a relieved heart, gave thanks to the only One who is able to both call and sustain the weary.

I wish I could say that from that day on, all my feelings of being done were stripped away, but that wasn't the case. I still had a lot of work to do. But what that day did do was remove the focus from the false solution I had created in my mind, which was moving back to America. That wasn't a solution; it was a lie I believed. The only solution to our brokenness is Jesus.

The devil knows our weaknesses. He knows what will make us unproductive and ineffective. Dissatisfaction with our job, marriage, or living situation can lead to dissatisfaction in the beautiful life the Lord has blessed us with. The enemy knows this.

Once I heard a sermon about blessings and walked away with the thought that if we have accepted Jesus as our Lord and Savior, then we are blessed to have our future in the heavenly realms. While we look for blessings in our spouse, kids, jobs, and more, we really should be looking to the One who has already given His all so we can have it all. Lord Jesus, please help me remember this when I begin to lose my focus.

CHAPTER 9

Called to Forgive: Surrendering to Grace

Bear with each other and forgive one another if
any of you has a grievance against someone.
Forgive as the Lord forgave you.

—Col. 3:13

This chapter has proved to be one of the hardest to write. I have come back to it again and again and found myself unable to finish it. I have invited the Lord to teach me what it is He wants to teach me about forgiveness. I have asked that His light would reveal any shades of darkness regarding forgiveness. I have opened myself up to both hurt and humility as I seek this in my heart. God is our example, and He tells us to forgive. I pray for His help to model this in my own life and in the depths of my heart.

Maybe you think you're the exception when it comes to forgiveness. I know the thought has crossed my mind a time or two. Then I return to God's Word and am reminded that there are no exceptions. Matthew 18 is a very convicting chapter on forgiveness. Maybe you've heard some of the story. Let's take a little peek into a scene between Peter and Jesus. Peter comes to Jesus and asks, "Lord, how many times shall I forgive my brother or sister who sins against me? Up to seven times?" (Matt. 18:21).

Isn't it amusing that Peter answered his own question? Do you ever do that in your own prayer life? Do you ask God a question, only to find yourself answering it? I bet Peter even thought he was being merciful by saying seven times rather than two or three. I am sure seven felt like a safe answer, but it wasn't.

In verse 22, we see Jesus's answer. "I tell you, not seven times, but seventy-seven times." I would like to have seen the look on Peter's face. Seventy-seven times! What? I wonder how many of us have had to forgive someone 77 times. Seems like it would get old. Then I think about my own sin and how many times the Lord has forgiven me. I assure you it is far more than 77 times 77. Praise Him for His example!

Matthew 18 also holds a treasure in a parable about forgiveness. Jesus tells a story about a man who owed his master a very large sum of money. The servant could not pay the debt, so his master ordered him to be sold with his wife and children and all that he had. The servant fell on his knees and begged his master to be patient with him, that he would return everything if he gave him time. As the story goes, the master felt pity for him and not only let him go but completely forgave him his debt. Isn't it interesting how the man's sin affected his whole family? That is how sin works. It affects everyone around us. Forgiveness is the same way. When we forgive others, everyone influenced by that situation is affected. So the wife and children and even the servant left their places of despair and went on about their lives.

Obviously, the servant had something other than thanksgiving in his heart because the story goes on to tell us that the servant went out from that place and found one of his fellow servants who owed him a fraction of the debt for which he had just been forgiven. I wish I could say that the forgiven debtor had learned his lesson and extended the same grace, but that was not the case. Instead, he demanded payment in full, and when the man could not pay, he threw him into jail. The bystanders were distraught at his behavior and went to the master who had originally forgiven the man's debt and reported all that had happened. The man who had his debt forgiven was thrown into jail with no mercy being shown. The chapter ends with a warning: "This is how my heavenly Father will treat each of you unless you forgive your brother or sister from your heart" (Matt. 18:35).

If we're honest, we have to admit we've all been in every one of the positions in the parable. We have all had the power to offer significant forgiveness. Maybe we did and maybe we didn't, but imagine that you *did* offer forgiveness, and the recipient essentially spit in your face by demanding payment from others, learning nothing at all from the grace you extended. We have also all been the person desperately begging for grace. It is clear that when it comes to our relationship with Christ, He is the master of all the debtors and offers forgiveness time and time again. Will we be those forgiven ones who freely learn from His example and offer forgiveness, or will we continue to condemn others?

Forgive as the Lord has forgiven. How did He forgive us? He forgave us enough to suffer and die for us. He took our place. He paid our penalty. The judge asked, "Who wants to die for these crimes?" Jesus, being innocent of all, stood up, raised His hand, and went to the cross for me and for you. And we need to forgive like *that.*

I have seen some pretty miraculous things happen in my life concerning forgiveness. I have also watched the effects of unforgiveness eat people alive. Sometimes it is ourselves we must forgive. Let me tell you that if Christ forgives us and tells us He has washed our sins away as far as the east is from the west, then what in the world are we doing *refusing* to believe His words? His sacrifice was enough. He is enough. His forgiveness is enough. Receive it for yourself.

The Lord has allowed me to witness my husband offering forgiveness to a man who was on the verge of suicide. The timing was perfect, although to our human minds, it made no sense at all. Josh's obedience to reach out and offer forgiveness opened the eyes of a man who later opened his heart to the Lord. Praise Him! I have watched a woman dear to me forgive her husband for having an affair. Her courage in that act could only come from the power of Christ within her. I will never assume that these valiant acts of forgiveness came easily, but they were liberating and God-honoring.

Forgiveness is not about feelings or emotions. It is not about a good idea or an inclination to do the right thing. Forgiveness is about obedience. Forgiveness is about surrendering, not to our will but to His will. He offered forgiveness, and we must follow His example. My children and I memorized this verse through song: "Bear with each other and forgive one another if any of you has a grievance against someone. Forgive as the Lord forgave you" (Col. 3:13).

When I think back on various parts of my life, I don't really remember having trouble forgiving people. I began to understand at an early age that to offer forgiveness to others was life-giving, and I've always wanted to be a life-giver. I have never had it in me to condemn, make others feel guilty, or shun, so the most likely path has been to forgive. I have struggled with expectations of hearing the words "I am sorry." Because those three words are generally easy for me to say, I expect them to flow freely from everyone—but that is not usually the case.

Several years back when we were in the States on furlough, I was doing a Bible study that rocked my world. I can't remember what the Bible study was or the author, but I do remember sitting on the couch in a little house we had come to love. That particular morning, the devotion was on forgiveness—again, something I did not struggle with and an easy step of obedience for me. That morning's introduction was a story about a father's forgiveness to the person who took the life of his son, written as a conversation on levels of forgiveness. Here's how I remember it.

"Do you forgive the man who killed your son enough to stop hating him?" was the first question posed.

The father, knowing the Lord, was able to answer honestly, "Yes, I can stop hating this man."

As the questions of examining the heart progressed in the story, the level of forgiveness also increased.

Next came, "Do you forgive him enough to tell him you forgive him?"

Again, the father responded, "Yes, I can tell him I forgive him."

"Do you forgive him enough to pardon his sin and encourage the courts not to send him to jail?" To me, that was getting a little deep, yet the father in the story continued to rise to the occasion and offered forgiveness.

The line of questioning continued. "Do you forgive him enough to pardon him, not send him to jail, and share the gospel with him, offering him eternal life? After all, isn't that what we are called to do?"

I vividly remember the physical sensation of nausea that overtook my body. My heart began to pound, and my breath quickened. In all my days of easily offering forgiveness, I had never thought to forgive the man who took my whole world from me as a little girl.

After reading all the questions and knowing the Lord was about to push me to apply this lesson personally, I began sobbing and rushed into the bedroom where Josh was sleeping. I knew what the Lord was asking me to do. I needed to forgive the man who had killed my father some 30 years before. But not only was the Lord asking me to forgive him, the Lord was also asking me to *tell him* that I forgave him and that if he would believe, Christ would forgive him, too.

Even as I write this, I recall my flesh screaming, *No way! What are you thinking? Leave that job to someone else.* Yet I knew in my spirit that the Lord had tasked me with this offering, this example of obedience to Him.

I wrestled with my thoughts for several days before I totally surrendered and committed to take the plunge. I talked it over with the Lord and asked Him to give me the strength I knew I would need to make it happen. I talked it over with Josh and asked him to help me follow through when it got hard. I talked with my grandmother and uncle, and they rejoiced with me over God being big enough to put this on my heart and encouraged me to follow through.

Finally, one day soon after, with a heart full of fear and hands that trembled, I picked up the phone and called the police station that had records on the details of the case. I was sent to voicemail where I left a message. "Hello, my name is Kristen. I am calling in relation to the case involving my father. I would like to contact the man who was convicted of his murder." I babbled on and on. When I hung up, I felt victory that I had taken the first step of obedience; but I really didn't expect anyone to return my call so soon.

When the detective called me back, I babbled on and on about who I was and what the Lord had asked me to do. He listened as I told him that I was a Christian and that I wanted to extend grace and forgiveness to this man as an act of obedience to the Lord. He understood my heart but then told me I would not be allowed to contact the man at the present time.

My father's murder had been classified as a cold case for the past 30 years. The evidence surrounding his murder was always considered circumstantial, although there was enough circumstantial evidence that my family and I felt certain we could identify the murderer. While the man has yet to serve a day of jail time in relation to my dad's death, he has spent the last 25 years in prison for another murder.

With the recent development of new forensic testing, advances have been made in the case. For the past 10 years, the police have been trying to get the case to trial. With the possibility of a court proceeding in the near future, any contact I would have with the man was not advisable. If I were to offer forgiveness to a man who is on trial for the murder of my father before his conviction, it would look like I was placing blame and trying to trap him in a confession. So I haven't seen him yet. When I think about him in my flesh, a fear comes over me, something that has been brewing for decades. However, when I look to the Lord, I know He goes with me and behind me and hems me in from all sides (Ps. 139), so whom shall I fear?

I have written my father's accused killer a letter, offering my forgiveness, but I haven't mailed it because of the legal issues that make it inadvisable. But even though he doesn't have the letter yet, I need to think of it as just what it is, an act of obedience. I don't necessarily understand it, but I trust the One who asked me to do it. I am thankful for His power to heal my soul. He is a good, good Father.

An old saying tells us that unforgiveness is the poison we drink, hoping the other person dies. That is true. To hold on to grudges and become bitter because the offender doesn't deserve to be forgiven is a recipe for disaster for our own souls.

Women have a tendency to convince ourselves that *we* don't deserve forgiveness. Why is that? We are sinners saved by grace who are going to mess up many, many times. Let's do the world a favor and pick ourselves back up. Let's be conquerors and not victims. The self-pity and self-loathing are getting us nowhere fast. We have been forgiven, so let's live like it. Let's live like free women. Let's surrender to the grace and mercy the Lord offers us by both giving and accepting forgiveness.

The story of my father's accused killer is a pretty drastic story of forgiveness. It was a true miracle the Lord performed in my heart, something I could not have done without His power and strength. But let's be honest. Even when our spouse makes those rude comments or our friends leave us out of the group chat, forgiveness can be about as easy as pulling teeth. Our pride raises its ugly head, and our heart screams that it's not fair. But why? Why is forgiveness so stinking difficult? I think the enemy places fear in our hearts, some lie we have believed somewhere along the way. I have a few I have to battle with—"Don't let them walk all over you!" "You deserve better!" "I would never do that to *them*; how could they do that to *me*?"

Recently, I wrote this in my journal after having my feelings deeply hurt by some people very dear to me.

> *I am so insecure sometimes. I let words hurt me. I believe lies. I forget who I was created to be and who I am meant to please. I don't like myself very much when this happens. I should be stronger than that, more rooted in Christ and His love for me. What signal does this type of weakness send to those around me? That I am mousy? A doormat? A weak person who lets the world stomp all over her and judge and condemn her until she feels backed into a corner and assumes a posture of defeat? Bondage. A slippery slope that I know is not of the Conqueror who lives inside me. Bondage. A well-rehearsed scheme of the enemy.*
>
> *Even though my flesh is insecure, I will hold on to the promises that God gives me in His Word. I will run to Him to heal my wounds and rearrange my thoughts. In my weakness, He is made strong, so I will boast in my weakness all the more so that His power may make itself known in my inner being. I am an insecure woman so Christ can be seen living in me. I let words hurt my heart so I run to the promises of His Word, which is life-giving and true. I will not be ashamed of who I am because I am a sanctuary for the Most High.*

I think that to be someone who easily forgives, we have to learn how to identify lies that we believe, debunk those lies, and replace them with truth. I wish I had a magic formula I could carry around in my pocket to reveal lies, or maybe a set of truth goggles that would show the wearer the world only as God sees it. Unfortunately, I don't have either, other than the Word, which is our goggles of truth, and I would never want to take away from the power of God's Word. From experience, I know without a doubt that it is super easy to spot lies that others believe, but it is *very* difficult to spot the lies that we believe. We can become blind to those lies, and everything becomes fuzzy and out of focus. I have learned and committed to memory 1 Corinthians 14:33, which teaches us that our God is not a God of confusion.

What does believing a lie have to do with forgiveness? Everything, in my opinion. John 8:44 tells us that Satan is the father of lies, and it is because of lies that we are unable to forgive. Let me explain. Your husband speaks a harsh word to you for no reason. You need to offer forgiveness, but you really don't want to. You begin to believe the lie that he doesn't deserve to be forgiven, that it is his job to seek forgiveness. After all, he was the one who wronged you. What lie exists in that argument? Do you see it?

We often misinterpret forgiveness as telling someone that their wrong action was okay or that we are letting them off the hook, but that isn't true. Offering forgiveness is an act of obedience commanded by the Lord Jesus who is the example for us all. The thought that your husband doesn't *deserve* forgiveness for speaking harshly is a lie created by the enemy to trap you into a life of bondage through unforgiveness. Forgiving others is freedom for the soul. That is truth.

I have experienced and witnessed firsthand the incredible destruction of believing a lie. It is crazy to me how innocent actions can be twisted and misunderstood when filtered through a lie. Let me give you an example that I recently observed. Someone in my life believed I didn't want them to be part of my life. It is not important how they came to that conclusion, but they did, and it was a big lie they believed. Because they believed this lie, they filtered everything I said and did through the filter of that lie, which created a complicated web of mistruths that seemed very real to them. Due to the lie they believed, it was easy for them to gather evidence to support that lie and add to the argument in their mind of how true it actually was. Only bringing these kinds of thoughts into the light and confessing them out loud will help us see clearly and be able to distinguish truths from lies.

CHAPTER 10

God's Provisions: Surrendering All Understanding

"For my thoughts are not your thoughts, neither are your ways my ways," declares the LORD. "As the heavens are higher than the earth, so are my ways higher than your ways and my thoughts than your thoughts."

—Isa. 55:8–9

W e've all heard the saying "God works in mysterious ways." We are told in scripture that His ways are not our ways, and His thoughts are not our thoughts (Isa. 55:9). It is such a gift from the Lord when something happens in our world that our earthly mind does not understand, yet we can see the hand of God at work.

We had been living in a particular city for many years, trying our best to be creative in reaching the people with the message of the gospel. One method we had been trying was offering English classes for anyone interested. The problem we ran into was finding the right location for our office. After renting a small apartment-type place on the outskirts of town, we were ready to move closer to holding the classes.

Looking through the advertisements proved helpful, and we found a really nice, even unique place in the very center of town. It was perfect. The only problem was the price. They were asking too much for monthly rent. We just didn't have it in our budget. Of course, our God is not limited by money.

The town we were living in had four walking streets that met at a huge circular center with a statue in the middle. One morning, we set up a table at the statue and passed out hats, scarves, and gloves, along with Bibles and other Christian literature in another attempt to get the message of the gospel to our city. It had been a very busy morning, and we'd had many great conversations with people about the love of God. The kids were there, running around, riding scooters, and doing their thing as the city bustled with people on this cold day.

In the middle of one of those spiritual conversations, Josh noticed a man who began to speak very loudly. Trying to press on, Josh did his best to tune him out. Our national brother was also quickly becoming aware of the situation. To not cause too much of a commotion, the men tried to engage the upset man in conversation. It was obvious that he was furious, saying we were a sect and had no right to pass out anything in his city. Our men tried to calmly explain that they were sharing scripture and books with God's truths, nothing more. It didn't take long for the scene to escalate, and before anyone knew what was going on, the man flipped our table over, throwing Bibles, hats, scarves, gloves, and everything else we had all over the ground. We were left in confusion, and the man quickly walked away.

What did we do? you may be asking. Well, my six-foot-four husband chased him down and made him come back to talk to the police (just kidding). We simply picked up our materials and carried on with the task the Lord had called us to do. We were shaken yet confident in this: "What, then, shall we say in response to these things? If God is for us, who can be against us?" (Rom. 8:31).

We had no idea that the Lord was already at work. That too-expensive apartment right in the city center had windows that overlooked that very place, and the landlord had just witnessed that entire scene. He quickly came out to where we were standing to speak with my husband. He said he had never seen someone act with such calmness and grace as Josh and our national ministry partner did. He went on to tell them that he would love to rent his apartment to men like that, for whatever price they could afford. For the last three years we lived in that town, we used that little place in the city center as a base to tell people of God's love for them. While the man who flipped the table intended harm, the Lord used his actions for His will to triumph.

God is like that, isn't He? He uses the everyday, ordinary things of this world to accomplish His goals. Even the sinner who means harm can be used by the Creator.

The end of the story has been written. God wins. The devil and all those who follow him *will* bow down to the King of kings and the Lord of lords. While the evil that remains in this world is heartbreaking, it is not a picture of the final battle, and I believe God is using it all in the tapestry of the story He is weaving for His glory.

Every time I sit down to watch the news, my heart aches. Children are being harmed, people groups annihilated, the sanctity of life constantly degraded—I could go on and on. Sometimes I think about those who ask how a good God could allow such evil to happen. For some, I realize they have simply chosen to believe a lie, and the evidence is piling up in their defense of this lie. The world is going to hell, and fast. But to those people who question the goodness of a God who allows tragedy to happen in the world, I want to respond not with a theological education but from a heart that is surrendered to Him. This world is not our home. Rest, dear friends, in the truth that God is good. "Taste and see that the Lord is good" (Ps. 34:8).

Events will take place in life that are not fair and do not feel loving—huge things that cause loss, betrayal, defeat, and despair.

Some people grow bitter during those storms of life. Some people just try to stay busy to avoid the issues, while others have learned how to talk the Christianese talk but inwardly question God. Living a life surrendered to God does not make you immune to these coping mechanisms because your flesh will still wage war within you. However, living a life surrendered to God will help you remember the truths found in His Word. "For now we see in a mirror dimly, but then face to face. Now I know in part; then I shall know fully, even as I have been fully known" (1 Cor. 13:12 ESV). Our trust is in God, not in our own understanding.

There will be times in life when suffering comes that you know God could change. You'll see unanswered prayers and many injustices in this world. When you are walking through these times of questioning God's goodness, remember that God loves you. Remember that pain can be profitable, and lessons can be gained from grief. Remind yourself that suffering is a result of the fall, and this world is not your home. Always trust God's heart. Knowing that you are not in control and that a loving God *is* brings freedom. Live in that truth.

I do believe that at any moment, the Lord Jesus has the power to return. Sometimes I ask why He hasn't. I do believe that God could stop children from being harmed, those innocent, precious children who are daily exploited and brutally harmed. Sometimes I ask why He won't. I do believe the Lord could give doctors a cure for cancer. Sometimes I ask Him why He waits. I do believe that God is stronger than all the evil that lives in this world. Sometimes I wonder why He doesn't stick up for His people.

Then I cry out to Him. I ask Him these questions and share with Him my hurts. I pray on behalf of the suffering and mourn for those who have lost. My anger turns to sadness, and my confusion turns to trust. I know my God, and He is worthy of all trust.

I don't know why He allows these things to happen, yet He does, and for me, that is enough. So while the world continues to go to hell, I will hope, and I will pray, and I will look for the goodness that He gives every single day. The forces designed to cause havoc, to flip our tables and shatter our dreams, are being redeemed by the Redeemer. He gives us beauty for ashes (Isa. 61:3).

I believe our job is to be a light in the situations He allows us to be part of. As believers, we are His hands and feet, and we have the power to bring Him into any situation, no matter how awful. When light enters a situation, darkness flees (John 1:5). So let's be lights in this world that doesn't make sense.

One of my favorite verses is Isaiah 26:3, which promises that God will keep me in perfect peace if my mind is steadfast because of my trust in God. The promise found in this verse helps me center my gaze on the only One who is worthy. Want peace? Keep your mind on the Lord. He is the peace-giver.

Sometimes I feel confusion, fear, and anxiety. Actually, I feel those emotions often. A few months ago, I was in a constant state of confusion. I wanted to hear the Lord speak to me, yet I felt as if I couldn't discern His voice. Hearing opposing thoughts caused me to remain confused. I was seeking Him with all I was yet walking away empty and confused. Almost in a state of panic, I went to the Word and found 1 Corinthians 14:33, which tells us that God is not the author of confusion but of peace. Obviously, the author of confusion is our enemy, Satan. Some distraction was causing my constant confusion and inability to hear the Lord's voice, but I was unable to identify the source.

Maybe you, too, are hearing some type of confusing noise. I want to assure you that it is not from the Lord. Our God is not a God of confusion. He is a good, good Father who wants the best for His children. All we have to do is go to Him with our questions, doubts, anxieties, and confusion. He loves the authentic and blesses the honest. Every. Time. He is worthy.

Life is messy. If I haven't conveyed that up to this point, then there you have it in print. Life is messy, and life is hard. Life is also not fair. I often speak that truth to my children. We must come to grips with the fact that not everything that happens to us in life is fair.

However, peace is possible even in the storms of life. We do have the choice to find joy and even laughter in times of trouble. Those of us who call ourselves believers have the choice to rest in the truth that the Lord is in control.

At one point, multiple spiritual attacks came our way. Looking back in hindsight, I can see the enemy trying his best to tempt and test us in all kinds of ways, but walking through the storm seemed like a breeze at the time. All I can say is that, sometimes, God in His goodness chooses to protect us. Because I have experienced it time and time again, I would even be so bold as to say that He does that on a regular basis; we are simply unaware of the battles going on around us in the spiritual realm.

At the time, we had Dayne, Abigail, Darcie, Josiah, and Jase, and we were on our way to Slovenia for a team retreat with five children. We had a several-hour drive ahead of us, but we'd made longer trips. Loading up the car for such an endeavor can be a challenge, but we've become pros. Kids and luggage were packed and loaded, and we were off.

The drive went fairly smoothly. I remember laughter, songs, and, as always, good conversation with my man. It wasn't until we got to a neighboring country that the out of the ordinary began to happen. To enter into any country in this part of the world requires a border crossing. You never know how long these events might take. You might get lucky and be waved through after 15 minutes, or you could be stuck at the border for hours or even overnight. Our crossing went just fine, but once we entered the country, we began to experience delays. At the time, we had no idea what was going on. We were in the middle of nowhere with open fields on all sides of us, rolling along on a four-lane highway minding our own business, when all of a sudden, we hit traffic—lots and lots of standstill traffic. Again, we had no idea what was going on, so we stopped and waited at least an hour.

We assumed there must have been a wreck until the same scenario played out again. We were in the middle of a huge highway in the middle of fields when we once again found ourselves in standstill traffic for another full hour—with *five* kids.

"Maybe it's not a wreck," we began to conjecture. By the third stop, we were pretty sure it had to be something besides a wreck. We had no idea what; we just knew we were two *very* tired parents with *five* very-ready-to-be-out-of-the-car kids.

We finally passed the third standstill and were traveling down the road with the windows down, trying to give the kids a little fresh air, when the car started acting a little funny. Josh immediately looked down. *Gas!* We were out of gas. We began to coast and pray. Remember, we were in the middle of nowhere. We could see fields all around us, and that was it. But the Lord was gracious, and our car rolled onto an exit ramp and stopped within walking distance of a gas station. God took such good care of us. The place where the car stopped was safe, and we didn't need to worry about being hit by oncoming traffic. Josh easily walked to get a can of gas. We could feel God's hand of protection on us at the time. Looking back, I can see even more clearly how much He protected us.

We went the rest of the way without any major problems and finally arrived at the team retreat location. That night at dinner, we were recounting our many delays. That's when we learned that old land mines in those middle-of-nowhere fields from the war in the late 1990s were being detonated. We should have known then that we were going to be "dancing in the minefield" for the rest of that weekend.

Thankfully, these particular incidents didn't seem as stressful as they could have. For whatever reason, we chose joy in those moments of inconvenience. Sometimes that comes easily and naturally; sometimes it is a very deliberate choice. I can think of a million times when minor inconveniences completely stole my joy and ruined my day or even my week. I believe that a big difference is our ability to learn to laugh and view life as a grand adventure; we must choose to make each turn an opportunity to build character and become more Christlike.

The team retreat was held at an indoor waterpark, and parents and kids alike had so much fun. However, we were there with five other families, and the interpersonal relationships were, unfortunately, a real struggle. Tension was high, and the elephant in the room grew larger with each meeting. While Josh and I were largely removed, we still felt the drama; our hearts ached for all involved. Again, it was a major opportunity to allow Satan to steal our joy, realign our focus, and put us in a position of living in the flesh. However, we continued to seek the Father and chose joy.

The enemy clearly saw that he was not going to lure us into his schemes with this interpersonal drama. We were rising above it and, honestly, keeping our distance. So Satan brought another attack our way.

The hotel where we stayed was quite unique in that the rooms were little individual cabins, cute and full of character. Each family had their own little cabin, all side by side. One night there was a horrible rainstorm with very strong winds, constant lightning, and hard rain. I have no doubt the Lord created this scene, and it was something beautiful that the enemy tried to steal.

I was up and down a lot throughout the night. Having a nursing baby and several children who were shaken by the loud storm made for a restless night. Not only that, but the roof in the kids' room began to leak water on their beds. By morning, we were all curled up in one queen-sized bed, all exhausted from a very restless night.

The next morning, I felt an uneasiness in my soul. At the time, I thought it was because of the chaos caused by the storm, but I would soon find out it was much more.

The morning brought bright sunshine, and Josh decided to get out of the little cabin and go for a morning run while I got the kids up and ready. He opened the cabin door and began chatting with a friend in the neighboring cabin when a realization struck him, and he asked, "Where is our van?"

Our friend pointed to the left and replied, "Right there." There it was, 500 meters from the driveway of our little cabin, 500 meters from the place we had parked it the night before.

In a moment of confusion, many ideas whirled through Josh's mind. He wondered if the wind of the storm had pushed it or if he had driven it and didn't remember. Just what in the world was going on?

He ran over to the van, and the answer became clear. Someone had tried to steal it. The thief had pushed down the window and snatched open the door. In an effort to get the vehicle started, he completely jerked out everything under the steering column. It was such a mess, and we would never be able to repair it completely. With the ignition and wiring harness torn out, we had to use two keys to crank the crazy thing for the rest of the time we had it.

We called the police, who told us when they arrived that this type of thievery was common here since it was near a bordering country that was part of the European Union. If they had succeeded in starting the van, they would have been free to drive it throughout the EU without stopping. Thankfully, due to the good ol' Volkswagen, they didn't succeed, but it was a nightmare trying to get all the wiring back together. God provided a place that made us a makeshift starter so we could drive it home. Later, Josh discovered that one of the police officers had stolen his paw-paw's pliers. Josh had checked the car door to make sure the thieves hadn't taken them and was relieved to find them where he had left them. Unfortunately, when he went to use them a few hours later, they were gone. He questioned the policemen, but they all denied taking them, of course, so there wasn't much else to be done. To this day, he can't talk about these events without mentioning those pliers.

We also were in a time crunch of sorts since we were going from the retreat to the airport just in time to pick up Josh's dad and his wife who were coming to visit from America. I was so nervous that the mechanic would have issues with making the van drivable in time, but he came through. We were at the airport just in time with a crazy story to tell.

Let's recap this wild trip. We had multiple hour-long delays in the middle of fields all because someone was blowing up landmines. Then we ran out of gas but made it to a station safely. We arrived to find our team embroiled in interpersonal conflict and very high tension. Then our car was vandalized and almost stolen. All of this happened in a matter of three days. When it rains, it pours. Everything happening around us was completely out of our control, but when I think back to that chain of events, I can almost imagine our family being inside a bubble of sorts, with the world swirling around us and our family maintaining a sense of peace and calm amid the chaos.

Life is like this much of the time. Chaos seems to be swirling outside and in all directions. Sometimes we feel like we can barely hang on, and other times we are oblivious to all the battles that rage around us. Regardless of how we feel, God is on the throne and remains all powerful. He does not waste our hurts. He is in our lowest of valleys and on our highest of peaks, and He has a purpose in it all.

The devil is real, and he is out to destroy anyone who exists to glorify the Father. He sends landmines, daily inconveniences, and interpersonal drama, and tries his best to steal our joy. He knows our stress points and weaknesses. He knows what works. He knows how to ignite the fears in our hearts that have long existed. He knows how to distract us with the logistics of life. He knows how to plant lies and bitterness in the middle of meaningful relationships. He doesn't hold back. He. Is. Pure. Evil.

But He who lives in us is greater than he who rules this world. "Little children, you are from God and have overcome them, for he who is in you is greater than he who is in the world" (1 John 4:4 ESV). And God is faithful. "God is faithful, who has called you into fellowship with his Son, Jesus Christ our Lord" (1 Cor. 1:9).

While we don't always understand God's ways or what He is up to, we have to learn to surrender our understanding to His authority and trust Him. Many today struggle with this question: How can a good God allow that to happen? Sometimes the answer is as simple as I don't know. Sometimes the answer is as complicated as I don't know. But there are many things we do know. God is good, and He reigns. Trust Him when the storms are blowing. Trust Him when the waves are still. Trust Him when nothing makes sense. Trust Him when all seems right with the world. Surrender to trusting Him.

CHAPTER 11

Your Body Is Not Your Own: A Surrendered Body

Do you not know that your bodies are temples of the Holy Spirit, who is in you, whom you have received from God? You are not your own.

—1 Cor. 6:19

God calls us to surrender our lives. Okay, check. I've got that. Most days. I at least have the understanding of what it means to surrender our ambitions, goals, and plans for our lives to the lordship of Christ. But do I actually surrender on a daily basis?

God calls us to surrender our thoughts. I understand that concept and work hard daily to be obedient and take those naysaying thoughts captive. But do I actually surrender on a daily basis?

God calls us to surrender our hopes and dreams. That is hard for me, but through faith, believing that His hopes and dreams for me are better than what my own feeble mind can come up with makes

90

that a little easier—some days, anyway. But do I actually surrender on a daily basis?

God calls us to surrender our marriage. As a woman who likes to feel in control, this can be hard for me. But through multiple circumstances, the good Lord continues to lead me to let go and let God. As much as I can have a good marriage in my own strength, God wants me to have a *great* marriage with Him tightly knit into our lives. A cord of three strands is not easily broken is a reminder to us from Ecclesiastes 4:12. But do I actually surrender on a daily basis?

God calls us to surrender our children. Whew! I could write an entire book on this one. He has been teaching me since the day they were born that they are not really mine; they are just on loan as a blessing. But God is in total control of their lives and destiny. It is my responsibility to shepherd their hearts straight to the Giver of Life, provide them with a godly home, and be an example to them as I live my life surrendered to God. But do I actually surrender on a daily basis?

All these lessons, all these layers, yet here is a new one for me. God calls us to surrender our bodies. Maybe this is old hat to you. You may be thinking, "Yeah, Kristen, don't you know that scripture says our bodies are a temple?" Yes, I know that verse. Here, however, is where I am going to camp out since this is a new refining the Lord is doing in my life. Do I actually surrender on a daily basis?

This is where I fell short and now have a major scar on my body and across my heart. But before I tell you about my disobedience in not surrendering, let me explain to you the circumstances surrounding my journey when I began to write about surrendering my body to the glory of the Lord.

As I write this, I am pregnant with my seventh child. Who has *seven* children? Me! Let me try to elaborate without being offensive.

This is just one honest woman walking through some fires as the Lord turns her into moldable clay.

This pregnancy was a surprise. You might laugh at that, as I am obviously well aware of how children are conceived. I also have to admit that our other two surprises were numbers one and two, so that means we planned four in between and haven't been surprised in more than a decade. It is a totally different experience to get that news when you are not expecting it. Now bear with me as I tell you that I selfishly did not want to be pregnant. I actually felt more strongly about not wanting to be pregnant than I did about having another baby. During pregnancy, the enemy tries to heap a sense of shame into my head. He uses whispers and looks. He uses well-meaning comments and very surprised reactions. He uses a part of me that I am trying to eliminate—the people-pleaser who wants everyone to like her. He uses any and everything he can to create a heart of shame, fear, and regret. And I could stay there. I could have a huge pity party and cry and feel sorry for myself and in my mind completely rationalize my selfish behavior, so I did. I sat in that place for weeks, and it was ugly.

I did not want to read my Bible, and when I did, I felt like I had attention deficit disorder and could not concentrate on anything. My mind raced. I literally felt nauseous when I would try to hide myself away in the prayer closet. I rationalized it by convincing myself that I was nauseated (which was true) and that I needed more sleep (also true) more than I needed to seek the Lord (which was a lie).

I talked to Josh about it and whined and complained. I talked to my friends about it and got their understanding and sympathy. I did not talk to God about it. After all, I knew His Word. I knew He was the One who had opened my womb. He was the one who came into the path of scheduling that vasectomy and interrupted *our* plans. I told myself that maybe the problem was that I was mad at Him. How could I complain to the One who was responsible?

We didn't tell people for months. It was close to Christmas, and we wanted to tell the kids for a Christmas present. It was a sweet time. Then we made the news official and put it on Facebook and received all kinds of responses from well-meaning friends or Facebook followers. "Congratulations!" "I knew you guys were not done!" "Really?" It felt better to get the news out. I could finally stop sucking in my protruding belly. With this seventh child, I began to show at seven weeks.

Then I wrote to a friend who has many more than seven children, and I asked for prayer. I whined and complained. I knew I was way more concerned about what other people thought about me than I was about having a baby. That part had been commonplace for that mama. She encouraged me to begin to say things like this: "If God thinks I can have one more, then who am I to say that I can't?" At first, I said it because that was what I should say, what people expected me to say, and then the miracle happened. I began to believe it! *Yes! It's true*, I told myself. *God is faithful, Kristen. You know that! Live in that. Stay there. Get your booty up in the morning, no matter what, and get into the Word. He is faithful. He is your rest.* And slowly, my heart let go, and my body became the temple it was meant to be, totally surrendered while growing my baby of completion.

That makes me think of sweet Mary. She was just a young girl. Some historians say she might have been only 12 or 13 when she found out she was going to be the temple to grow our Lord Jesus. I wonder about all the emotions she experienced. Was she afraid? Happy? Honored? Naive to the reality of what life was about to look like? Probably all the above.

But do you know what she said? Mary said, "I am the Lord's servant. Let everything you have said happen to me" (Luke 1:38 ISV). This young woman is an example of a surrendered body, a surrendered life. The whole of history would have been changed without her attitude of servitude. While she knew that what was about to happen was pretty important, it's unlikely that she ever truly grasped the significance for all humanity. Maybe we as Christ followers still don't fully understand the magnitude of Immanuel, God with us (Matt. 1:23).

Let's look to Jesus as an example of a body surrendered. Paul talks about this in his letter to the Philippians.

> *Do nothing out of selfish ambition or vain conceit. Rather, in humility value others above yourselves, not looking to your own interests but each of you to the interests of the others.*
>
> *In your relationships with one another, have the same mindset as Christ Jesus:*
>
> > *Who, being in very nature God, did not consider equality with God something to be used to his own advantage; rather, he made himself nothing by taking the very nature of a servant, being made in human likeness. And being found in appearance as a man, he humbled himself by becoming obedient to death—even death on a cross!*

—Phil. 2:3–8

Talk about an example to follow! Jesus should be our example at all times. If we truly have the mind of Christ, doing nothing out of selfish ambition or vain conceit (wanting it to be about us), then a surrendered body is easy. If we remain in an unhealthy pattern of people-pleasing and other coping mechanisms, we are never going to live in the freedom Christ offers. As we learn to look outside ourselves to the interests of others, our minds will be blown at what a change of perspective can do for our overall health. Each time I get down in the dumps, it is a result of looking inward, feeling sorry for myself, or wallowing in discontentment. Thankfully, I have a man who can usually spot my inwardness and encourage me to look outward. Serve others. Walk with them through their problems. Share the gospel. It's a way to refocus and get my eyes on Jesus—and it works every time.

That is what Jesus did. Even though He was God, he became a servant. Even though He wore heavenly crowns, He became flesh. Not only did He become flesh, but He became obedient flesh, or surrendered flesh. He was hated, accused, beaten, and killed for no fault of His own but because He loved us so much. Living a life surrendered to the purpose of God is the example Jesus sets for us to follow.

So why, oh why, do I pitch little fits about things that interfere with my plans? It's because I want my way, and the most ridiculous thing about that statement is that I *know* His ways are better. So where does the misalignment happen? How do I lose my sight and focus? It happens because we are living inside flesh and blood in a very broken world, which is why we must daily surrender our minds, souls, and bodies to the lordship of Jesus Christ.

In less than 20 weeks, I will hold this little surprise miracle blessing in my arms and praise the Lord who opens the womb. In six months, I will not be able to imagine life without my brood of seven. His plans are always better than our plans. His ways are always better than our ways. His thoughts are always better than our thoughts. Doesn't it say that in His Word?

> *"For my thoughts are not your thoughts, neither are your*
> *ways my ways," declares the LORD.*
> *"As the heavens are higher than the earth, so are my*
> *ways higher than your ways and my thoughts than your*
> *thoughts."*
> —Isa. 55:8–9

Come on, old feeble and fickle flesh of mine, remember this truth when life comes knocking at your door. Hang tight to the life-giving words He gives as you navigate through this life. I will teach this baby, along with all my other children, that the world is full of lies calling us to surrender to them. Take hold of the only truth that exists—the truth that we are children of the living God who has a plan for us. He has a plan for us to live a life full of purpose and worth for the only One who is worthy.

I wrote the previous section when I was pregnant and waiting on baby Levi Allen to be born. He is a little over a year old now and the joy of our lives. God knew that we needed his sweet little presence added to our family. I do, however, want to share a very vulnerable part of my journey. My heart in sharing this is to allow God to use my hurt and even disobedience however He sees fit.

While I talk about surrendering your body to the lordship of Christ, I stand as a fallen servant. When I began this chapter, I see now that I was talking more about surrendering your plans and your mind to be happy and content with what God has planned for you, to lay down the mental space it occupies. I was referring to being a vessel for God to work through and doing so with a joyful heart. What I did not realize was that the big test of surrendering my body was yet to come. And I failed.

My first four children were born naturally—Dayne, Abby, and Darcie in America and Josiah in a large hospital overseas. Baby number five, Jase, came into the world in a very small, private hospital overseas by C-section. I grieved over that choice for years since the C-section was very unnecessary; but it happened. This made Emma, baby number six, an automatic C-section since she was born in the same small, private hospital as well. When it was time for baby number seven to be born, we were on furlough in the States. It was so sweet to think about having a baby in America around family and friends. The day of his birth was so special since everyone was there to welcome him into the family.

From the day I first found out I was pregnant, I told Josh, "This is my last; I am getting my tubes tied." He didn't love the idea, but I think he understood what I was saying in a way. I felt justified in that decision because my last few pregnancies, although not as horrible as some people's, were not enjoyable. I am so ungrateful in my flesh. Anyway, I had this same thought process for months, but then I really began to wrestle with it. *Should I get my tubes tied? Should I not? God, what do You want me to do? Is our family complete? I want our family to be complete.* I spoke with doctors. I spoke with family. I spoke with friends. I spoke with pastors. And yes, I spoke with the Lord. However, something in me was stubborn and hard. I wanted to be done. The world would tell me, "You should be done. Seven children are enough. Think about your body." My mind was being transformed to hear the voices of the world.

For years, we had planned a road trip out west with the kids during our last summer in the States, together as a family before our oldest went off to college. It was kind of a now-or-never deal. I just wasn't supposed to be pregnant, so Josh let me make the final call about whether we were still going to pull it off. It was a monumental trip, and I was going to be 34 to 38 weeks pregnant during the five weeks on the road. That is *really* pregnant. And for the record, the last three of those weeks were spent tent camping. Not that we give away mom awards and not that I need to toot my own horn, but I think I deserve a tough mom award for those three weeks of walking to the bathhouses, cooking on a tiny camping stove, and hauling six kids 8,000 miles in a van. Honestly, we had a blast and I loved *almost* every second. I am truly grateful that we gave the gift of those memories to the kids and to us.

We had been on the road for a few weeks and were speaking at a church in Oklahoma one Sunday morning when, during worship, I heard from the Lord. He told me to *wait*, and I knew immediately that He was telling me to wait to have my tubes tied. I began to cry, like ugly cry. Josh was wanting me to get it together as we were about to go up on the stage. He continued to look at me, and I knew

I had to tell him what God was doing in my heart. Through muffled tears, I was able to spit out, "God wants me to wait. I can't get my tubes tied yet." He just gave me a hug and said, "Okay." He knew that was not the answer I wanted from the Lord. He knew I wanted permission to be done with being pregnant.

We continued our road trip and had so much fun. Nights were pretty hard for a very pregnant mom sleeping on a cot, but I made it work. I had some significant pain in my right leg, but I thought it was just from sleeping on a hard cot for so long.

As the days and weeks went by, it seemed I looked for anything and everything I could to stop hearing God's instruction to wait. I tried to forget it. I tried to tell myself that I didn't hear it. I began to listen to the desires of my heart rather than the desires of the Lord. Then I began to bargain with the Lord. *Lord, if you just let me go into labor naturally, then I will know You don't want me to have my tubes tied.* Because we were in the States, they would have allowed me to have a VBAC (vaginal birth after Cesarean). That would have been an easy answer—just allow my body to have that baby naturally, no cutting required, no Cesarean, no tubal ligation. That was my plan.

I was scheduled for my C-section at 39 weeks on a Monday. Early in the morning on Sunday, July 22, the day before my scheduled Cesarean, I went into labor. Around 7:00 a.m., Josh drove me to the hospital. Sure enough, I was in labor and already dilated four centimeters. My sweet Jesus did everything He could to try to convince me to wait. It was probably around 7:30 a.m. that I was given a choice—and I chose wrong. I chose disobedience. It is one of those moments in life that you replay in your head time and time again with such ache and regret in your heart. The nurse came in. "It says on your chart that you are thinking about having a VBAC. Do you want to try to labor or go ahead with the Cesarean and the tubal ligation?" All I had to do was choose the natural route. It was the fleece I had put out before the Lord. If only I could relive the next few hours, countless nights of lying in bed full of regret and countless hours of mulling over my act of disobedience would have been avoided. If only I had listened to God's "wait."

"I want my tubes tied, so let's go ahead with the C-section" is what I said. And that's what I did. Levi was born, and while he was a grumpy little fellow, he was perfect. In the operating room, the doctor asked me once again, "Are you sure you want to proceed with the tubal?"

I replied, "I already have seven children. Yes!"

"You have such a beautiful uterus; are you sure?"

"Yes, I am sure," is what I said, to my shame. I can still smell the burning of the flesh.

The grief I have experienced since that decision is unexplainable. The regret hurts so much that it makes me feel nauseated. I have no idea of the blessings our family will miss out on because of my act of disobedience. God may have planned for our family to have several more children. Maybe Levi was the one who completed our Hepner family, but I will never know for sure. However, I do know for a fact that I chose disobedience.

January 12, 2019

It comes and goes, this open wound. This scar that I cannot get to go away. This disobedience that haunts me. Earthly voices all pointed to one answer, the answer I wanted, but the voice, the only One that matters, sweetly said, "Wait." He whispered, "Wait," and I heard, and I obeyed, and I told three of my closest friends, knowing that I would be weak. And I was. I was weak. I chose what I wanted. I chose the way that made sense. I chose wrong. And I can't help but wonder what would have been. What blessings will I now miss out on because I was disobedient? And my heart aches. And I feel shame. And I am sad. But the Voice, the same One, again whispers, "My grace is sufficient," and the yoke lightens, and I can breathe,

---

> *and peace comes. Then He sends a word to me; He sent it days before. I've been chewing on it, thinking it was for another loved one, waiting to share the truth with someone else. But right now I realize, I realize He sent it for me for this moment, and I let it sink in. "Healing can flow from a wounding."*

The wound my act left is beginning to heal, but I will forever have a scar. It is beginning to heal because the Lord has already forgiven my sins, even this sin of disobedience. He tells us in His Word that He has removed our sins as far as the east is from the west, and we are forgiven (Ps. 103:12). The hard part is forgiving myself. While I have begun that process, it will take a while. I will continue to speak God's promises to myself until I believe them, because they are true. Romans 8:28 tells us that God can use all things for good to those who are called according to His purpose. Jeremiah 29:11 assures us that He has a plan and a hope and a future for us. Isaiah 43:25 promises us that He will not remember our sins, for His *own* sake. His promises are true and right, and I will rest in them.

A sweet sister recently told me, "God is allowing you to grieve through this so you will know to listen to His voice next time." My heart cries out in response, "I don't want a next time. I want to be obedient *this* time. I want to undo the wrong that I've done."

The reality is, what is done is done.

Maybe you have a regret in your life that haunts you. It might be something you've replayed over and over in your mind that you would give anything to change. You dream about it night after night and want to wake up from the distress you feel. Some things you can fix or change, but others are permanent, never to be undone. God is still God. God is still good. God still loves you. If you have breath left in you, He is not done using you for His glory. Don't disqualify yourself. Learn from your mistakes, and continue to surrender your life to the only One who is worthy.

CHAPTER 12

Grace under Fire: Surrendering during the Unexpected

*And his name—by faith in his name—has made this
man strong whom you see and know, and the faith that is
through Jesus has given the man this perfect health in the
presence of you all.*

—Acts 3:16 ESV

If you were to create a good person category, I would be in it. If you knew me, you would probably like me, and if you didn't, unfortunately, I would care. It makes my heart happy to see people smile and to be an encouragement to others. I go out of my way to try to love on all those around me. It disturbs me to think that I could possibly offend someone with a glance or an unintended misspoken word. I like to be liked, and I like to be a good person.

However, that good person category goes out the window when we start to talk about the salvation of our souls. It is not enough for God that we are good people. He wants us to have hearts fully surrendered to the lordship of Jesus and lives dedicated to following Him. The Bible says He searches the earth to strengthen those whose hearts are fully committed to Him (2 Chron. 16:9). I believe He allows us to walk through very difficult and unexpected seasons with this strengthening of mind.

We had just settled into our overseas home after returning from several months of being in the United States for our furlough assignment. I had yet to fully unpack from the attic what we had stored up there for safekeeping during our absence. The life we have been blessed to live can sometimes seem less than ideal, but that's looking at our circumstances through a glass-half-empty lens. No one will disagree, however, that the logistics of living overseas, especially with such a large family, can be a nightmare. Therefore, when things happen, such as the events that were about to unfold, life gets complicated. A stressful health situation became a complete life change, a physical move, and the uprooting of nine people.

When I really think about it, I realize that the pain began during my last pregnancy. Remember that camping trip and sleeping on the cot? I attributed the nagging and increasing pain in my right hip and leg to that. When I became unable to sleep well due to the pain and then the struggle of mothering seven children while sleep-deprived began to affect me in very real ways, I knew I had to get help. The pain felt like sciatica. My mom has a bad back from herniated disks and a host of other problems, so I assumed genetics and the years were catching up to me. At the beginning of 2019 when the pain began to disrupt my sleep, I determined I needed to try to find some help and relief. I found a few physical therapists in our town and went many times for various treatments. They used electricity, ultrasound, and magnets, and gave me certain stretches to complete, all in an effort to alleviate the pain. Some days I had hope that the treatments were working, and then the pain would return. This cycle went on for months, and I was exhausted.

Looking back, it was a sweet time for me spiritually. Due to the lack of sleep, I would begin most mornings watching the sun rise with my heart and soul in the Word. Jesus was my only refuge. The suffering my body was going through pushed me to the throne of grace morning after morning. I am grateful for those hours sitting in my chair with the Lord. He was preparing my heart for what was to come.

On Thursday, April 4, 2019, I had an MRI. For the past year (and maybe more), Josh had been faithful to fast and pray every Thursday. This spiritual discipline is something I so admire in him. That particular day, he was prepared for the battle that was coming. I had my first panic attack while I was in the MRI machine. I had never felt a physical reaction to anxiety before that day.

During the MRI, I knew something wasn't right when they stopped the process to put dye into my veins. I knew something wasn't quite right when I saw the radiologist's face. I was more than grateful that he spoke English, one of the many provisions my sweet Jesus gave me. He was blunt and frank and kind and sympathetic when my tears came. Josh wasn't with me, but Jesus was.

I'm sure you've heard people say their world stood still. It's true. That is what happens when you hear the words, "You have a tumor." I cried. The doctor was kind and quickly explained all that he could. "You have a significantly large tumor inside your spinal cord. You will need surgery. I think it would be best for you to return to America." It felt like a dream.

I walked to the car, crying. I didn't understand exactly what was going to happen, but I knew it was bigger than I wanted it to be. I called Josh and prepared him for my crying self that was about to arrive home. Josh was calm and took control. The Lord had completely prepared him for this moment of uncertainty. Josh called his mentor who is in a leadership position in our organization. We were uncertain about how to proceed. Thoughts of plane tickets, see-ya-laters, the logistics of moving nine people, a house to stay in, surgery, cancer, finances, and so much more proved to be a lot for me. I was, well, useless for those 10 days when Josh tied up a few loose ends, packed as if we were going on a two-week vacation, and got us all on a plane.

God was so faithful in those days to give us extra amounts of grace and to open our eyes to the provisions He was showering on us. After one particularly hard day, I woke up in the middle of the night to a panic attack. In an effort to turn off my mind, I looked at my phone to see a message from a friend telling me to look up Exodus 14:14. Reading the words felt like Jesus Himself was speaking to me. "The LORD will fight for you; you need only to be still." I slept like a baby, waking the next morning to news that answered my heart's deepest desire at the time. It was a strong, tangible confirmation that the Lord had complete control over the situation. It was also the beginning of my own personal understanding of how out of control I am in my own life.

I am convinced that a great work of the enemy is convincing us to be self-sufficient and to believe the lie that we control our lives. As believers, we may be in control of our hearts, maintaining self-control, remaining teachable and other internal attitudes, but it is the Lord Jesus who controls our lives. And the Bible clearly informs us that God's ways are not our ways, and His thoughts are not our thoughts (Isa. 55:8–9). When things happen to us that are life-altering, we usually get a dose of humble pie in the realization that we are not in control of our lives.

What I know now is that neurological pain caused by a tumor has no rhyme or reason. You have good days and bad days. When I had electricity therapy, sometimes a good day would follow, and I would become hopeful that it was working, only to go again to the same therapy and have a bad day afterward. I was so frustrated and honestly becoming a little hopeless that pain would be a constant in my life. At one point, I had become convinced that I was dealing with piriformis syndrome (Google told me so). I began to do stretches every day and walk, and that really seemed to help a lot. Then it stopped working. At that point, I decided I needed to have an MRI, mostly because if I had a disk problem and continued all the stretches, I could make it worse. All I wanted was some pain relief, to be able to play soccer with my boys, and to get back to the gym with my man. I was becoming frustrated and losing all hope that my life would ever be the same.

Don't we do this all the time in life? We become discouraged to the point of losing all hope. There is a truth in Jesus that hope does not disappoint (Rom. 5:5). When we put our hope in anything but the Lord, we will be disappointed. I've personally been guilty time and time again of putting my hope in myself, my husband, my job, the next vacation, finding pain relief, and the list goes on. It is all in vain; we are chasing the wind (Eccles. 1:14).

After the radiologist's report of finding the tumor, we felt certain we needed to see another doctor. The radiologist had said we needed to see a neurosurgeon. With a full heart, Josh tried to go about his normal routine. At the gym, he saw a good friend named Johnny who was actually my physical therapist and very invested in my health. With a heavy heart, Josh shared the news of the tumor and our very likely trip to the States. Johnny took the news hard. As with most Balkan people, he had a great desire to help in any possible way; so later that day, he made a phone call to a friend and former colleague in a nearby city. Johnny told this friend my story and shared with him our desire to see a doctor to confirm the radiology report. Since we don't believe in coincidences, this was one of the first small miracles God used to bring glory to His name. Johnny's friend was sitting in the office of the lead orthopedic surgeon in the country, the same surgeon who had saved Johnny's life many years before. This man subsequently agreed to see me the following morning. Johnny called

Josh with such joy and awe that this connection had been made and that I would be able to see a very seasoned doctor the next morning.

I will always remember that drive. We were so full of peace and questions. It was a very paradoxical feeling. I even had a small amount of hope that the test results were all wrong and there really was no tumor. The surgeon, a very kind older man, confirmed the presence of a large tumor inside my spinal cord and told us that it needed to be surgically removed. We left his office and drove home, making plans for how to move mountains and get our family the help we needed.

Here is an entry I made in my journal on the day after they initially found my tumor:

> *Jesus, You know, even better than I, that I have eight people who depend on me. Jesus, may this also teach them to depend more on You. Jesus, please heal my body. Jesus, please send us to the right place, the right doctors, the right hospitals. I feel that this journey will be longer than I would like, but I trust You every step of the way. Even today, please give us peace in the waiting. This morning as I seek Your face, just to be with You, please draw near. I need You more than breath. Be near my loved ones. They need You, too. Josh is being strong. Give him places and people where he can be weak.*
>
> *Jesus, You just spoke the sweetest promise over me—Acts 2:25–28. I like the NLT version the best. "I see that the Lord is always with me. I will not be shaken, for he is right beside me. No wonder my heart is glad, and my tongue shouts his praises! My body rests in hope. For you will not leave my soul among the dead or allow your Holy One to rot in the grave. You have shown me the way of life, and you will fill me with the joy of your presence."*

As God often does, He moved every mountain that stood in our way. Within 10 days, we had everything we needed—nine plane tickets, availability in the mission home we always stayed in (where my children felt at home), a vehicle that would hold all of us (that we had decided not to sell six months earlier), and a loving family and church family waiting for us. The body of Christ is so beautiful in times of crisis. We felt completely loved and supported on so many levels during that time.

Leaving our Balkan home and walking into the unknown was hard. This is a journal entry from the week before we left:

> *As I sit in "my chair" this morning and look out "my window," my mind trying to read the very last pages of* Breaking Free, *my eyes keep looking out "my window." This is my safe place, my home. I see my swing and the kids' swings and their bikes. The blooming Japanese magnolia tree, the vine that has begun to grow, the dandelions sprinkled on the ground—and I wonder where I'll be next week. Stability and security are gone—we are walking into the unknown completely by faith. It's overwhelming, yet I feel more alive than ever. No way to numb this reality. No covering it, no dodging it; it's real and before us, so, Lord, give us the strength we need for today. Truths I am learning: suffering brings you into a more intimate relationship with Jesus.*

I praise Jesus for His provision of the body of Christ that awaited us in the States. Without the hands and feet of Christ, the struggles of this world may have stolen our peace and our joy. However, all of us, from Josh to baby Levi, remember this very difficult storm with fondness due to the community that surrounded us, on both sides of the ocean.

Are you in community? Do you have a brood of people who know and love you well? A Sunday school class? A life group? If not, you are missing out. It is so important to build strong relationships with others in the body of Christ because when life gets hard, you are going to need them. God intended it that way. His people are His hands and His feet. We have never felt more loved and cared for by Jesus because we were so connected to His body of believers. Don't miss out on experiencing God that way. Get plugged in.

The next five weeks were hard—very hard. I had most of my emotional meltdowns in the morning. My best friend pointed out to me that this was because mornings were the time I had patterned my life to be with Jesus, and He wanted to be with me during my meltdowns. I loved that thought. So most mornings, Jesus and I would take all the lies and fears and squash them.

It took several weeks to find a neurosurgeon who was willing to do the surgery since it was pretty complicated. It then took another couple of weeks to complete further tests, including additional MRIs. At one point, doctors questioned whether the known tumor was the only tumor. There was even talk that it could be coming from my brain. Those days were very scary since Google had me convinced that I had only five years to live, and I was not okay with that. Josh and I were becoming very familiar with the possible outcomes—relearning how to walk, losing complete control over bowel and bladder functions, and even possibly total paralysis. We were okay with all those scenarios, but we were never able to accept the possibility of my death. It just wasn't an option.

During this time, I was most concerned for Josh. I knew I would be okay. I would go to sleep and wake up to deal with whatever the Lord decided the outcome would be. However, I worried that Josh would be a nervous wreck for the duration of the surgery. I was very thankful afterward for the many people who came to the hospital to provide a distraction for him.

Talk about some intense feelings and conversations! It was a sweet time of getting perspectives in line with what really mattered. Josh and I were fighting together, and we knew the battle was worth it. My journal entries throughout this time were full of scripture verses, God's promises, and lists of things for which I was thankful. It was a very uncertain time, but I knew Who was certain, and I clung to Him.

The kids were doing well through all the transition and chaos. They absolutely love our church, so they were enjoying reconnecting with their friends. The older children did their schooling online, so that was not interrupted. The younger ones enjoyed playing in the yard and seeing family. Baby Levi transitioned back to the States well, but my heart ached for him, knowing that I would have to wean him early due to all the medicine that would go into my body for the surgery. Overall, the kids were coping just fine. One of my middle daughters, Darcie, who is my right-hand person, had many fears and worries about her old mama. The morning of my surgery, when it was still dark, she woke up to hug me and pray over me, and she cried as I left. I was so proud of her faith in Jesus that He was going to take care of her mama.

The journey we had taken up to this point was full of unknowns, and our future was very uncertain, yet we remained strong. We had no clue what our future held, but we had complete faith in the One who held our future.

After fully explaining the risks involved, the doctor scheduled and performed my surgery. Josh still gets chills every time he tells the story of the doctor coming out of the operating room. I always imagine the doctor rushing toward Josh with a huge smile on his face and saying, "I just watched a miracle." He explained to Josh the anatomy of the spinal cord and where the tumor was in relation to how it is made. Apparently, we have a "straw" around the spinal cord, which is mostly a thick substance until you get to the midback where the spinal cord branches off into fibrous nerves they call the horse's tail. My tumor was at the exact spot where the two meet, under the thick, fibrous material and down into the horse's tail. It was a very delicate surgery, but the doctor was amazed at how the tumor seemed to peel away. Working very gently, he was able to remove 100 percent of the mass. Though four pathologists were on site, none of them could identify what the tumor was, so off it went to the lab.

God gave me a precious nurse in recovery, and I remember waking up and crying. I remember asking if the tumor was gone, if my legs worked, and if I could see Josh. I couldn't open my eyes because I couldn't focus. My eyes were jumping around the room thanks to all the medication I'd been given.

By the time Josh arrived at my bedside, I was crying even more, probably due to a combination of the anesthesia and relief. He was there with me the first time I moved my toes. The doctors already knew I was not paralyzed because they did neuron monitoring during the entire surgery. The doctor explained to Josh that when they hooked me up to the monitor before surgery, my right side was almost completely nonresponsive. He was surprised I was able to walk presurgery. God protected me. I know He did.

Two nerves in that horse's tail were badly compromised—squished and stretched almost to the breaking point—but they held together by a tiny string. God protected them. I know He did.

Before they took me out of the operating room, my neuron monitor lit up like a Christmas tree, according to the doctors. That's when they knew I would be fully functional after the surgery. I am a medical miracle. God protected me. I know He did.

We celebrated many firsts after my surgery. The first time I woke up, ate, sat up, used the bathroom, and walked down the hall. We walked into that storm with absolutely no idea what life would look like on the other side, and we walked away as if nothing had happened. God gave many promises and scriptures in the days following my surgery. I recorded my favorite in a Facebook post I sent out to the hundreds of people who were praying me through.

But I am like a green olive tree
*   in the house of God.*
I trust in the steadfast love of God
*   forever and ever.*
I will thank you forever,
*   because you have done it.*
I will wait for your name, for it is good,
*   in the presence of the godly.*

—Ps. 52:8–9 ESV

Jesus gave me this promise the week before the surgery while I was at the beach. I've been holding tightly to "I will thank you forever, because you have done it" (Ps. 52:9). And indeed, He has done it. He protected me and the intricacy of my spinal cord nerves. I am truly fearfully and wonderfully made. There is nothing better to be than a green olive tree in the house of God. I've had peace and strength and joy, not because of who I am but because of where I'm planted—in the Lord. May His name be highly praised, and may all rejoice for what He has done! Thank you for every prayer you prayed for me! Together we watched a miracle!

It was truly almost unbelievable that I was walking the day after my surgery, riding a bike 22 miles two weeks later, and on a plane headed overseas six weeks post-op. God just wanted me to include this incredible journey as part of my story, and I love it. I am so thankful for the stories He is writing in and through me. He is the Great Physician and the best author.

Conclusion

I appeal to you therefore, brothers, by the mercies of God,
to present your bodies as a living sacrifice, holy and
acceptable to God, which is your spiritual worship.
Do not be conformed to this world,
but be transformed by the renewal of your mind, that by
testing you may discern what is the will of God, what is
good and acceptable and perfect.

—Rom. 12:1–2 ESV

I t is hard to even write the word *conclusion* because this story is far from over. God isn't done writing His beautiful story of my life. I am excited to see what the next 20 years will hold and whether He will allow me to write and share those events. In the meantime, my heart's desire is to live out the verses above, to live every day as a sacrifice to God with a heart full of worship, to fight against my flesh and the rushing river of culture, to renew my mind with the patterns of God and His truths, to be tested and refined until I look more and more like Jesus, to discern the will of God and walk in it, to do what is good and acceptable and perfect, to live a life surrendered to Jesus.

Surrendering your life yields so many benefits. I pray that my stories have challenged and encouraged you to get to know Jesus in a more intimate way and to learn to surrender *everything* you are to Him.

I have never for one day regretted any decision I've ever made to be obedient in following Jesus. While it was not always easy and often very hard, I have never regretted it for a second.

Surrendering my life to the lordship of Jesus has allowed me to live a life bigger than myself. In our immediate and self-centered society, this way of thinking about day-to-day activities remains very countercultural. It will take some work. It will take learning disciplines and establishing rhythms in your life that will stretch you as a person. But it will make you a better person—one you will be proud of.

Living a life of surrendering will free you from living a life full of worry about your future. You may not know what your tomorrows will look like, but because you know the God of tomorrow, you have no need to fear. We have an eternity to look forward to with those we love, worshiping the only One who is worthy.

Acknowledgments

Writing this book has proved to be so much more of a blessing to me than I ever thought possible. Of course, I pray it was also a blessing to you, the reader, but ultimately, I feel it was God's gift to me. Years ago, I had the idea to get some of these stories into words so my children would always have a memory of what the Lord has done in our lives and would see visible pictures of His goodness. That leads me to where I would like to start giving thanks.

To my Lord and Savior, Jesus, the author of my story and lover of my soul, thank You. Thank You for the uncountable gifts and blessings You continue to shower on our family on a daily basis. Also, I want to thank You for the overwhelming joy You have placed in my heart as I write these words of Your goodness. It has been the joy of Your presence and the act of worshiping You through my writing that has helped this dream become a reality.

Have you ever met someone who not only saw the gifts and talents in your life but also had the ability to pull them out of you? I am privileged to be married to such a hero. Years ago, he began to push me toward this endeavor of writing a book. Over the past few years, he has encouraged and applauded every step. Without you, Josh Hepner, I fear my story may have been boring. You make life interesting and an adventure. Thank you for always believing in me and loving me like you do.

Dayne Gabriel, thank you for always reminding me that I have the supernatural ability to make you always feel like my favorite. You have been around to watch so many of my triumphs and failures, yet you love me through them all. Abby Grace, thank you for reading my words, taking them to heart, and encouraging me by being inspired by them. Your presence in our family brings such depth and richness in so many ways. Darcie Ann, this book would not be here without your constant help of being my right-hand woman. I pray with all my heart that I will be able to return the favor to you one day in your own family, though I doubt anyone would ever be as blessed as I to have a daughter like you. Josiah David, you are such a blessing to this mama and really all who know you. Your servant's heart to help and your inquisitive mind to learn inspire me and reveal that God has great plans for your life. Jase Isiah, your goofy smile and loud noises make our home so much fun. Having you around helps my heart stay young and my soul laugh on a daily basis. Emma Joy, my little princess, we named you right since you radiate with joy. As I watch you grow and dance and become such a lovely little girl, my heart squeezes with longing to hang on to every minute since I have learned they go by too fast. Finally, my Levi Allen, God's sweet blessing to my stubborn heart. I am more grateful for your sweet smiles and curly blond hair than words could ever say. My prayer for all seven of you is that each and every day you will live deeply, surrendering all you are for all He is. Lord, may it be so.

To my family, Mom and Bob, Mema, Papa, Shanna, Granny, Lee, Adam, Christina, and everyone in between, thank you. Thank you for loving me and our family in a way that allows us to be who we are where we are, knowing we have your full love and blessing. This is a gift you will be repaid for in eternity. We will never be able to match the depths of your love this side of heaven.

To my girls Randi, Steppie, Katy, Sunshine, and Amy, thank you. Thank you for loving me and allowing me to be real and honest, broken and redeemed. Thank you for your encouragement over the years and cheering me on to what God has called me to.

Samantha, you came into my life just three years ago, but from day one, I knew you would be one of my biggest fans. I have deeply appreciated your encouragement and words of affirmation. Angie, thank you for your time and help editing this very novice writing. You helped me create something I am proud of. Jeremey, thank you for being available one Wednesday afternoon, encouraging me on my journey and giving me great insight into so many things.

Without that one Skype call, Lucid would not be part of this journey. To everyone at Lucid, thank you for every message, phone call, email, and tireless minute you put into making *Surrendering* the best it can be.

To all the ladies who read my very first, very raw copy and still encouraged me to keep going, thank you. Heather, Karen, Michelle, Susie, Elisabeth, and Angela, you ladies read my manuscript, believed in the message, agreed to associate your name with it, and cheered me on in my journey. Your kindness and the time you spent doing that are much appreciated.

Finally, thank you to my readers. The joy that overwhelms my heart to think that I was able to spur someone on in their walk with the Lord is unfathomable. Thank you for taking your time to read my stories. I pray you have been encouraged to continue *Surrendering* every aspect of your life to Jesus.

Questions to Ponder

Chapter 1: My Story: Unaware of Surrender

1. If someone were to ask you to share your story, where would you begin? How is that significant?

2. I defined the word *peripeteia* as a sudden or unexpected reversal of circumstances or situation especially in a literary work. Viewing your life as a story, where do you see the peripeteia in your life?

3. Read Matthew 11:29, and rewrite the verse in your own words.

Chapter 2: Our Love Story: Cords of Surrender

1. Describe a difficult time in your life that you now see as a blessing.

2. Whether you are married or not, you have most likely heard marriage advice in your lifetime. What is the best marriage advice you have ever heard, and why?

3. Psalm 103:12 is a powerful promise. Take some time to write a prayer of thankfulness and tell God what it means to you personally.

Chapter 3: My Call: Surrendering to Obedience

1. Do you know how to transition your own story of salvation into a gospel presentation?

2. Describe the difference between making God your Savior and surrendering to Him as Lord of your life.

3. Read the story of Jesus and Peter in Matthew 14:22–33. In what areas of your life is Jesus calling you to "get out of the boat"?

Chapter 4: The Land of Milk and Honey: Surrendering Dreams

1. How would you describe your relationship with Jesus?

2. What are some selfish dreams that you have had to surrender or lay down?

3. Read James 1:2–4. What specific trials are you facing? Are you living out what James says in these verses?

Chapter 5: God Can Use Anything: Surrendering Idols

1. What special ability, talent, or character trait has the Lord blessed you with? Are you using your gifts and talents to bring glory to God?

2. What are some idols that tend to sneak into your life repeatedly and steal your joy?

3. Rewrite this scripture and replace the bold words to make it personal.

   "**Each of you** should use **whatever gift** you have received to serve others, as faithful stewards of God's grace in its **various forms**"(1 Pet. 4:10).

   For example, mine would be "Kristen, you should use the gift of writing to serve others, as a faithful steward of God's grace through writing books, creating blog posts, and encouraging others through His words."

Chapter 6: As a Servant of the King: Surrendering Desires

1. Do you agree with this generalization: "We are a lot like children when it comes to learning to delight ourselves in the Lord"? Why or why not?
2. Name some ways that your heart and soul delight in the Lord.
3. Rewrite Psalm 37:4 in your own words.

Chapter 7: He Makes It Okay with Your Heart: Surrendering Family

1. Think of a time in your life when you were able to see God's faithfulness in a personal way. Think about that time and say a prayer of thanksgiving or write about it in your journal and thank God for His goodness.
2. Do you find it more difficult to surrender control of your own life or the lives of your loved ones?
3. Jeremiah 29:11 was referenced a few times throughout the book. What do you think the scripture means?

Chapter 8: Reconfirmation of the Call: Surrendering Again and Again

1. Read the following passage from this chapter:
   "The enemy is sly. He knows how to plant enticing thoughts that don't really seem sinful to begin with but can quickly turn into disgruntlement, dissatisfaction, and sin."
   What seemingly innocent thought seems to pester you often, leading you to dissatisfaction with your circumstances?
2. Have you ever felt that you hit rock bottom in your life? Reflect on that time and remember how God brought you through it. Write a prayer of thanksgiving for both the hard time and the lessons learned.
3. Write Philippians 4:10–13 in your own words, and then underline the words that specifically speak to your heart.

Chapter 9: Called to Forgive: Surrendering to Grace

1. After reading this chapter on forgiveness, did the Lord prompt your mind to a specific hurt or a person you need to forgive?
2. What lies are you believing that prevent you from having a forgiving heart?
3. Memorize 1 Corinthians 14:33.

Chapter 10: God's Provisions: Surrendering All Understanding

1. If you are honest with yourself, do you struggle with finding peace? Does anxiety plague your thoughts?
2. What are some ways you have successfully learned to cope with worry and anxiety?
3. In the Chapter 9 questions, you were asked to memorize 1 Corinthians 14:33. Write what you remember. If you do not have it memorized, look it up and write it down.

Chapter 11: Your Body Is Not Your Own: A Surrendered Body

1. What parts of your life are you still holding on to, unwilling to fully surrender?
2. Are there mistakes from your past that continue to bother you? Are you hanging on to the guilt of disobedience or sting of sin surrounding this circumstance? List some truths you can cling to that point your heart back to truth.
3. Read the story of Mary from Luke 1:26–56. Describe Mary's attitude to having her life interrupted.

Chapter 12: Grace under Fire: Surrendering during the Unexpected

1. Many people struggle with control. Our culture teaches us at a young age that we are in control of our lives and our futures. But what does scripture say about who is really in control (Luke 12:22–26)?

2. Are you invested in a community of believers through your local church? Do you know others' hurts and burdens? Do you feel comfortable enough to share your own? If not, why not? If you are in a community of believers, describe what these relationships mean to you.

3. Read Romans 12:1–2. In what ways are you living out those verses? In what areas do you need to surrender more to Jesus?